The Look-It-Up Book of
MAMMALS

Patricia Lauber, formerly editor-in-chief of a young people's science magazine and Chief Editor, Science and Mathematics, for a leading children's encyclopedia, is the author of many books for children. She has written three LOOK-IT-UP Books, and has contributed several titles to two other Random House series, Allabout Books and Gateway Books. A graduate of Wellesley College, she now lives in New York City.

Guy Coheleach studied art at the Cooper Union for the Advancement of Science and Art. Since 1963, he has concentrated on wildlife studies and has contributed to various textbooks, an encyclopedia, and several other books. His work also appears regularly in National Audubon Magazine. He now lives in Astoria, New York, with his wife and four children.

The Look-It-Up Book of
MAMMALS

by Patricia Lauber
illustrated by Guy Coheleach

Random House New York

*We should like to thank
Ernest P. Walker, Mammalogist Extraordinary,
for his thorough reading of the manuscript
and his most helpful comments.*

What are Mammals

A grizzly bear is a big creature that walks on land. A bat is a small creature that flies through the air. A blue whale is a giant that spends its whole life in the sea. In many ways these animals are very different from one another. But in certain ways they are alike, for they all belong to the large group of animals called mammals.

All mammals have backbones. All breathe air. And all are warm-blooded. But these facts alone do not make them mammals. (Birds are also warm-blooded, air-breathing animals with backbones. Yet they are not mammals.) Two things are true of mammals that are not true of any other kind of animal.

1. Mammals have fur. Some, such as the musk-ox, are very furry, indeed. Some, such as the elephant, have only a sprinkling of bristly hairs. Some, such as the dolphin, have hair only when they are born. But no other kind of animal has any fur at all.

2. Mammals nurse their young on milk. Mother mammals have special glands in their bodies that produce milk. No other kind of animal does. The very word "mammal" comes from a Latin word for "breast".

Almost all mammals bear living young. But two kinds lay eggs. These are the platypus and the spiny anteaters. Some baby mammals are carried inside their mother's bodies until they are well developed. Others are tiny when they are born and have hardly developed at all. Most of these finish developing in their mother's pouch. This is true, for example, of kangaroos and opossums.

Most of the animals we know best are mammals. Dogs, cats, horses, cows, mice, monkeys, elephants, sheep, deer, and beavers are all mammals. And, as you may know, we are mammals, too. In this book you will find most of the mammals you know—and some you don't know. You will see what a surprising and wonderful group of animals the mammals are.

Aardvarks

Aardvark

An aardvark is a wonderful digger. Its strong legs end in huge claws. The aardvark uses its claws to dig the big burrow in which it lives. It uses them to dig out food—termites, ants, and other insects.

Aardvarks live in many parts of Africa. Some African termites build huge nests of earth above ground. The nests are as hard as concrete. An aardvark can easily rip open a termite nest with its claws. Then it eats the termites. An aardvark has a sticky tongue that reaches out for 12 inches. It gathers termites on its tongue and swallows them. Aardvarks hunt for food at night. They sleep in their burrows by day.

Their chief enemies are lions, leopards, and other meat-eating animals. An aardvark fights by rearing on its hind legs and slashing with its claws. It cannot bite. An aardvark has no teeth in the front of the mouth. The side teeth are peg-shaped and have no roots. An aardvark tries to escape from an enemy by running away or by digging a hole. It can dig a hole very quickly. Then it vanishes into its hole.

A female aardvark has one baby a year. By the time it is 2 weeks old, the baby can go out with its mother at night. At 6 months it is big enough to dig for itself.

The name "aardvark" means earthpig. Aardvarks look something like big pigs. But they are not pigs. In fact, they have no close relatives.

Alpacas
See Llamas

2

Anteaters

Giant Anteater

The GIANT ANTEATER is a large animal with a bushy tail and a tube-shaped head. It has no teeth. Its mouth is simply a small hole at the end of the snout. Inside the mouth is a long, sticky, wormlike tongue. When feeding, the anteater pokes its snout into a nest of ants or termites. Then it flicks out its tongue. Insects attack the tongue and stick to it. Then the anteater swallows them. It may eat a pound or two of termites at one meal.

An anteater rips open a nest with its claws. The claws are long, sharp hooks. They also serve as weapons. If attacked, an anteater stands on its hind legs and claws its enemy. Because of its claws, the giant anteater must walk on its knuckles. It can gallop if it must. It can also swim. The giant anteater has no fixed home. It spends its time shuffling around with its nose to the ground, looking for food. A mother carries her baby on her back.

The giant anteater has two smaller cousins: the COLLARED ANTEATER and the SILKY ANTEATER. Another name for the silky anteater is the PIGMY ANTEATER.

All three kinds are found only in Central and South America. The smaller anteaters spend much of their time in trees. They are active mostly at night.

Several other animals are also called anteaters. Among these are the SPINY ANTEATERS and the SCALY ANTEATERS, or PANGOLINS. All eat ants and other insects in the same way. But they are not related. The closest relatives of the American anteaters are the armadillos and the sloths.
See also: PANGOLINS; SPINY ANTEATERS

Collared Anteater

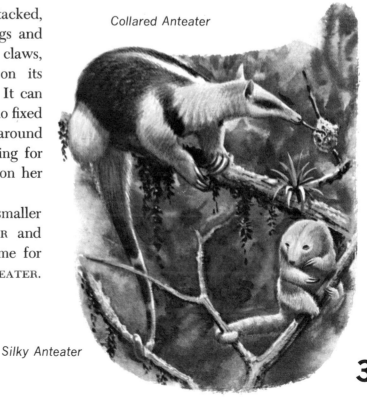

Silky Anteater

3

Antelopes

Antelopes are graceful, handsome, swift-footed animals. There are about a hundred different antelopes. They come in many sizes and colors. Some live in big herds, while others live alone. Some kinds live in thick forests. Other kinds live in scorching deserts, in swamps, on mountains, or on open plains. All are Old World animals, and most kinds live in Africa. (The pronghorn of North America is sometimes called an antelope. But it is not a true antelope.)

All antelopes have hooves. All are plant-eaters. When feeding, they swallow their food quickly. Later, when they are resting, they chew their cud. That is, they cough up the food, a mouthful at a time. They chew it thoroughly and swallow it again.

Antelopes have horns. Horns are hard and hollow. They grow around cores of bone on the skull. Horns are not shed, as antlers are. In some kinds of antelope, both males and females have horns. In

Gnu

Oryx

Springbok

Gazelle

4

other kinds only the males have horns. In general, antelope horns grow up from the head and then sweep back. But some are as straight as spears. Others grow in spirals or in great curves.

The biggest antelope is the ELAND. A male eland may be 6 feet high at the shoulder and weigh 1,200 pounds. Elands live in small herds on the plains and grasslands of Africa. The smallest antelope is the ROYAL ANTELOPE of West Africa. It is only about 10½ inches high at the shoul-der. Between these two are all the other sizes of antelope.

GAZELLES are small, graceful antelope of desert regions. The ORYX, which also lives in deserts, has horns like spears. The tiny DUIKERS live in the forests of Africa. So does the rare and beautiful BONGO.

On the plains of Africa you can see many kinds of antelope—HARTEBEESTS, GNUS (or WILDEBEESTS), SABLE ANTELOPE, SPRINGBOKS, and many others.

Impala

Kob

Eland

Duiker

Apes

Gibbon

Chimpanzee

Gorilla

Orangutan

Apes and monkeys belong to one of the main groups of mammals. The name of this group is primates, which means "first." The scientist who named the group said that it was first in importance. He thought so because man is also a primate.

All told, there are about 190 kinds of primate. Except for man, apes are the most highly developed. They are among the most intelligent of mammals.

There are four main kinds of ape: GIBBONS, ORANGUTANS, CHIMPANZEES, and GORILLAS. Gibbons are fairly small. The other three are big. That is why they are called the "great apes."

Apes do not have tails. (Most monkeys do.) They have big jaws and large front teeth. They eat chiefly plant matter—fruits, buds, leaves, and so on. Their eyesight is good, and they can see colors.

Apes are very good at swinging through trees. They can grip the limbs with their hands or their feet. Their feet look much like their hands and the big toe works like a thumb. The great apes also spend a good deal of time on the ground. They cannot swim.

All apes are Old World animals. Chimpanzees and gorillas live in Central Africa. Orangutans live on the islands of Borneo and Sumatra. Gibbons live in Southeast Asia, Sumatra, Java, Borneo, and some smaller islands.

GIBBONS are the smallest of the apes. They stand 3 feet high and weigh 12 to 18 pounds. They have very long arms. In fact, their arms are longer than their legs. A gibbon has a very loud voice. When feeding, it gives low, whistling cries. These are sometimes followed by shrieks and hoots.

On the ground a gibbon hurries awkwardly along. It is most at home in a tree. It is an amazing acrobat. Using each hand as a hook, the gibbon swings from branch to branch. It can swing from one branch to another that is 30 feet away. It can also walk along a tree limb. It grips the limb with its big toes and holds its arms up for balance.

A baby gibbon travels through the trees with its mother. It clings around her waist. She lifts her legs to hold it as she swings.

Gibbons

ORANGUTANS are much bigger than gibbons. A male may be 5 feet tall and weigh 220 pounds. These apes spend much of their time swinging through trees. They can also walk on the ground. When they travel on the ground, they use the sole or side of each foot and the knuckles of their hands. They sleep at night on a platform or nest of limbs. They usually build a new one each night. In rainy weather orangutans cover themselves with large leaves.

These apes are usually gentle and peaceful. But if upset, they are very dangerous. Few animals dare to attack them.

Orangutans seem to be very intelligent. They may be as intelligent as chimpanzees, but it is hard to tell. Unlike chimpanzees, they do not love to show off what they have learned.

See also: CHIMPANZEES; GORILLAS

Orangutan

Armadillos

Armadillo

Spanish explorers of the New World discovered many kinds of animals. Among these was one in armor. The Spaniards named it the armadillo, meaning "little armored thing."

As we know today, there are about 20 kinds of armadillo. And some of them are not very little. The largest is the GIANT ARMADILLO. It is 5 feet long from the tip of its nose to the tip of its tail. It may weigh as much as 120 pounds. But some others are small. The smallest of all is the FAIRY ARMADILLO, which is about 5 inches in length. It has pink armor and white fur.

An armadillo's armor is made of horny plates, or shields. They cover the back and sides. The head and tail are also armored. The underside of the body is furred. The back armor is divided into bands, or rings. Skin between the rings serves as hinges. It lets the animal bend. Some armadillos can curl up into a ball when threatened or attacked.

Armadillos are found chiefly in Central and South America. One kind is found in parts of the southern United States.

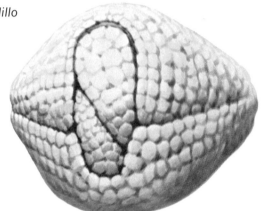

An Armadillo rolled up

This is the NINE-BANDED ARMADILLO. As you can tell by its name, it has nine bands in its back armor. It is about the size of a house cat. This armadillo cannot roll itself up in a ball. If alarmed, it moves very quickly. It hides in thorny bushes or in a hole. It is a good swimmer and can also walk across the bottom of a stream.

Nine-banded armadillos sometimes live in groups. They share a burrow that they have dug. They are most often seen at dusk or at night. They come out then to hunt for insects, small snakes, frogs, and other small creatures. A mother usually has a litter of 4 babies. They are all the same sex and look exactly alike.

Asses

See Donkeys

Baboons

Baboons are the largest of the monkeys. A baboon stands 2 to 3 feet tall and weighs between 30 and 90 pounds. These big monkeys spend their days on the ground. They walk on all fours and run in a rocking gallop. At night they sleep in trees. They sleep sitting up.

A baboon spends its whole life sur-

Mandrill (rear)   Mandrill (head)

rounded by other baboons. Baboons live and travel in troops. Such groups can defend themselves against enemies better than a single animal could. There may be 15 to 200 baboons in a troop. Each troop has its own area where it lives. Here it finds water and food. Baboons eat mostly plant food such as grass, fruits, buds, and tender shoots. They may also eat insects, scorpions, birds, and small mammals. By day the troop moves around, feeding and resting. At rest the baboons gather in small groups. Some baboons simply sit. Others groom one another. One picks through the fur of another with its hands. It removes dirt and ticks.

When the troop moves on, the males are at the outside. Meat-eating enemies cannot reach the females and young. An enemy meets the males, who are very brave and very strong. Most meat-eating animals have learned to leave the baboons alone. Only leopards and lions attack them. And only leopards and lions can make baboons take flight into the trees. Baboons often mix with other plant-eating animals. They feed and drink with elephants, giraffes, antelopes, and zebras.

A young baboon rides on its mother's back when the troop is moving. When the troop is resting, it plays with other young baboons. They chase one another, pull tails, and pretend to fight. If a young baboon gets hurt and cries, older baboons come running and stop the playing.

All baboons live in Africa. They have some close relatives there, called MAN-DRILLS and DRILLS. These large monkeys are startling in their looks. Their faces and seat pads are brightly colored. A male mandrill's face is purple, blue, and bright red. His seat pad is red-purple. If you see a mandrill in a zoo, you will remember it well.

10

Badgers

The badger is probably the fastest digger in North America. If it needs to hide, it digs with all four feet. The earth flies, and the badger vanishes from sight. Then it plugs up the hole behind itself.

The AMERICAN BADGER is a member of the weasel family. It is found from southwestern Canada to northern Mexico. It lives in open country—on plains, prairies, and deserts. It makes its home in a burrow that it digs. In spring a female badger builds a nest of dry grass in her burrow. Here the baby badgers are born. Usually there are 2 in a litter. At first they nurse. Then the mother brings them food. Finally, they follow her on hunting trips. Badgers eat rats, mice, rabbits, birds, snakes, lizards, eggs, and insects. They hunt at night.

If a badger catches something as big as a rabbit, it digs a special burrow. It takes the food into the burrow and stays there for several days. When it has eaten, it moves on. A badger never stays long in one burrow. So it is busy digging a large part of the time. Usually it lives alone. In autumn northern badgers become very fat. They hibernate, or sleep away part of the winter.

About 8 kinds of badger live in the Old World. One of the most interesting is the HONEY BADGER, or RATEL. It lives in Africa and Asia. The honey badger is a fierce fighter. It attacks animals much bigger than itself. Its skin is so tough that a dog cannot bite through it. Also, the skin is loose. The badger can twist inside its skin and bite an enemy that is holding it by the back of the neck.

The honey badger is very fond of honey. In the hot parts of Africa there is a bird called the honey guide. When it finds a bees' nest, it gives a certain call. The badger follows the call and breaks open the nest. Then the badger eats the honey and the bird picks up the crumbs.

American Badger

Bats

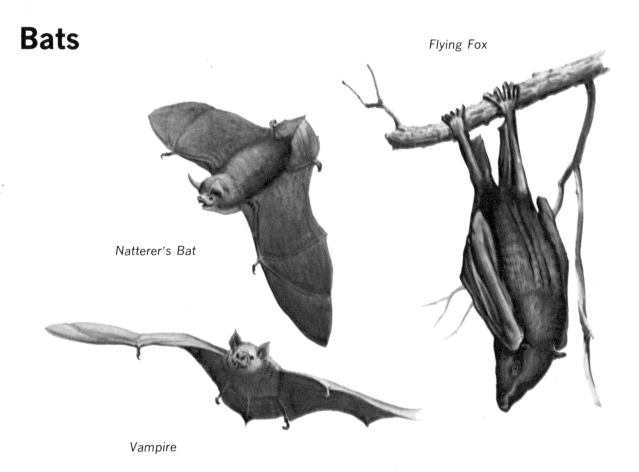

Flying Fox

Natterer's Bat

Vampire

Bat wing

Bats can fly. They are the only mammals that can. A mammal like the "flying" squirrel does not really fly. It glides from tree to tree. Bats are the only mammals that travel through the air with wings.

A bat has a furry, mouse-sized body. Its wings are made of skin that is stretched over bones. The bones are the bat's arms and fingers. The fingers are very long and slender. Only the thumb is not part of the wing. The thumb is short and usually ends in a hooked claw. A bat uses these hooks for climbing.

There are nearly 1,000 kinds of bat. Bats are found almost everywhere except in cold regions. Most are active only at night. That is when they come out to feed. Most kinds eat insects, but some kinds eat fruits. Some prey on frogs, mice, and other small animals. Some feed on the pollen and nectar in flowers. The VAMPIRE BATS feed on blood. They make a small cut with their teeth in the skin of a sleeping animal. Then they lap up some blood.

North American bats eat mostly insects. Sometimes they hunt insects on the ground. More often they capture in-

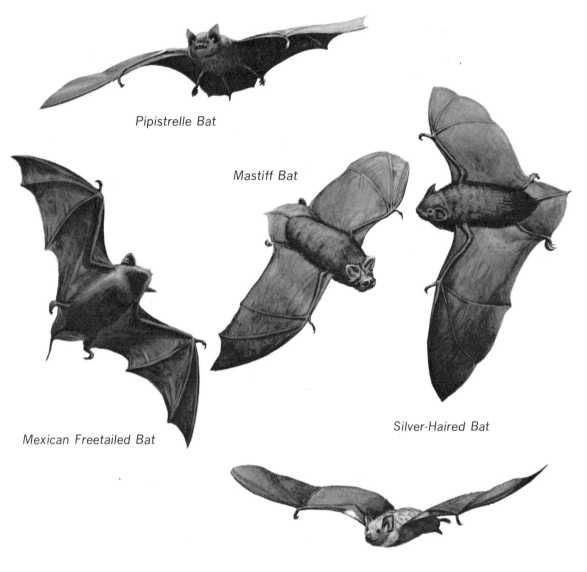

Pipistrelle Bat

Mastiff Bat

Mexican Freetailed Bat

Silver-Haired Bat

Hoary Bat

sects in the air. A bat may catch an insect in its mouth. Or it may "net" one with its wing or the pocket of skin near its tail.

Bats can see at night. But they do not use their eyes for hunting. They use their voices and their ears. A flying bat sends out a steady stream of sounds. Usually the sounds are so high-pitched that human ears cannot hear them. The sounds bounce off insects. The bat hears the echoes and catches the insects. Echoes also keep the bat from flying into things in the dark.

Most bats live in colonies. A small colony of 10 or 12 bats may live in a hollow tree. A large colony of thousands may live in a cave. A bat usually hangs itself up by the claws on its hind feet, but it can hang by its thumbs. It may hang from a

Bats coming home to roost

twig or branch. It may hook into a crack. It is usually head-down or upside down.

Bats cannot live in cold places. Some bats fly hundreds of miles to winter in a warmer climate. Other bats spend the winter in deep caves, where it does not get very cold. These bats go into a winter sleep. They hardly stir until spring comes.

Baby bats are born in late spring or early summer. A mother bat makes a cradle of herself. She hangs by her feet and thumbs, belly-up. The newborn baby rests in this cradle. Within minutes the cradle is no longer needed. The tiny baby can hold onto its mother's fur, using its teeth and claws. It travels with her when she flies off to feed. When the baby becomes too heavy for its mother, it stays home at night. The mother returns at dawn and feeds the baby. By the time it is 6 to 8 weeks old, the young bat goes hunting itself. It may live to be 17 or more years old. Bats have few enemies. Many live to die of old age.

Bears

Bears are big animals with stubby tails and thick legs. They are heavily built, but they can move very fast if they must. A bear can gallop at nearly 30 miles an hour. Bears are usually peaceful animals. But they are very dangerous when they are angry.

Spectacled Bear

Most bears live in the Northern Hemisphere. Only one kind lives south of the equator. This is the SPECTACLED BEAR of South America. There are four main kinds of bear in North America: black bears, grizzly bears, brown bears, and polar bears.

The AMERICAN BLACK BEAR is not very well named. Only some black bears are black. Others are yellowish, silvery, tan, and cinnamon-colored. One litter may have cubs of several colors. In one small area of southeastern Alaska, the black bears are silver-blue. On islands off British Columbia, they are creamy white. Black bears are found as far north as Alaska and as far south as central Mexico. They are the smallest North American bears.

Bears spend most of their time searching for food, eating, and sleeping. The black bear likes to eat meat best, but it cannot catch big animals. It eats mice, chipmunks, pocket gophers, and woodchucks, as well as fish, birds, eggs, and insects. It fills up on berries, fruits, grass, roots, bark, and bulbs. In summer and autumn the bears stuff themselves and become very fat. Cold weather makes them sleepy and they disappear into their dens. Here they doze away the winter. Around January the bear cubs are born. Usually there are 2 or 3 in a litter. They are born with their eyes shut and are very small. The mother bear goes on dozing, and the cubs nurse.

When spring comes, the mother takes

Black Bear with cubs

Beaver

anywhere from a few feet long to more than 100 feet. It is usually 1 to 4 feet high.

Beavers build dams to block streams and make ponds. A beaver needs a pond that is at least 2 to 3 feet deep all year round. In its pond a beaver is safe from enemies. And it has a place to store food.

The beavers usually build a lodge, or house, in their pond. They may build at the edge of the pond or on an island. The lodge is made mostly of branches plastered with mud. It has an air hole in the roof, but the entrances are underwater.

Once the lodge and dam are built, the beavers keep busy repairing them. As they drag branches over the ground, the beavers wear down paths. These are called "tote roads." Sometimes they dig canals from the pond to the tote roads. Then logs can be floated and towed.

Usually you will find a family of beavers living in a lodge. The family is made up of the mother, the father, and the last two litters of young. Just before a new litter is born, the two-year-olds are driven out of the lodge. They are now able to live on their own. The father also leaves for the time being. In late spring 3 to 4 baby beavers are born. The father moves back in. And family life starts again.

In summer beavers eat many kinds of water plants, grasses, roots, and herbs.

Beaver house

Beaver dam

They also eat tender bark, leaves, and buds. They store branches underwater for winter food. When the pond freezes over, the beavers swim under the ice to the food supply. They cut off a branch and take it to the lodge. When they have stripped off its bark, they throw it out.

Beavers have been much trapped for their fur. At one time they became very rare. Now they are protected by law. They are seen again in many parts of North America.

Bison
See Buffaloes

Boars
See Pigs

Bobcats
See Lynxes

Buffaloes

Bison

Indian Water Buffalo

The AMERICAN BUFFALO is a huge, shaggy beast with a hump on its shoulders and horns on its head. A bull stands 6 feet high at the shoulder. He can weigh up to 2,000 pounds. Buffalo are usually timid animals, ready to run when they see or smell you. But you cannot count on this. Sometimes a buffalo is bold. It lowers its head and charges.

Buffalo belong to the big family of wild cattle. They live on prairies and in open woodland, where they eat mostly grass. They like to be near water. They need water to drink. They are good swimmers. And in summer they like to wallow in mud. Wallowing helps to get rid of biting flies.

Bulls, cows, and calves graze together the year round. A cow usually has a calf in May. The calf is a lively little creature. It plays tag and follow-the-leader with other calves. It butts its fellows and pushes head-to-head.

At one time huge herds of buffalo roamed North America. There were per-haps 60 million of them. Early settlers and hunters slaughtered them. By 1890 only 500 were left. Fortunately, these buffalo were not killed. They were saved and bred. Today there are several thousand buffalo in the United States and more in Canada.

The American buffalo is sometimes called a BISON. This is its scientific name and a good one. It sets the American animal off from some others that are called buffaloes.

One of those is the WATER BUFFALO of Asia. It is a heavily built animal with curved, pointed horns. In the jungle it fears no living thing and fights fiercely. But it is often bothered by insects. To escape their bites the water buffalo may plaster itself with mud. Or it may escape into water. It stays there for hours with only its nose showing. The water buffalo has been tamed in some countries. It is used as a beast of burden and to pull plows and carts. It is gentle with people it knows but not with strangers.

The one-humped ARABIAN CAMEL is a desert animal. Its nostrils are slits; they can be closed to keep out sand and dust. Thick lashes keep sand out of its eyes. Its hoofed feet are broad and cushioned on the bottom; they are suited to travel across sand. The camel can eat almost any kind of desert plant. If it must go without food, it can for a few days. The hump on the camel's back is a store of fat. The camel's body can draw on the fat for food. Camels need water and will drink even salt water. But if they must, they can go without water for a few days. No one understands exactly how camels do that.

Arabian camels are sometimes called "ships of the desert." With a load of 400 pounds on its back, a camel moves steadily across the desert. Its long legs eat up the miles for hours at a time.

One-humped camels are found in the Near East, the Middle East, and North Africa. None live wild. They all belong to men. Men use them for riding and for carrying goods. Men also get milk, meat, wool, and hides from camels.

The one-humped camel is often called a DROMEDARY. It has a two-humped cousin called the BACTRIAN CAMEL. The Bactrian camel lives in central Asia. There are still some wild Bactrian camels, but many are owned by men. The two-humped camel is easier to ride. A shorter, heavier animal, it is slower than the one-humped camel. It lives in a colder climate and has longer fur.

Arabian Camel, or Dromedary

Bactrian Camel

Caribou

See Reindeer

Cats

The cat that purrs in your lap is a loving pet. But its body is very much like the bodies of the big cats that live wild. Big or small, all cats are made the same way. They are made for hunting.

A cat has keen senses. It hears well and smells well. Like all hunters, it has eyes that look straight forward. (A cow, for example, does not.) In bright light the pupils of the eyes are slits. At night, when the cat hunts, the pupils open wide. They let in much more light. (The eyes also reflect light. That is why a cat's eyes shine in the dark when they catch a gleam of light.)

Dogs are runners who chase their prey. Cats hunt in a different way. They may quietly track their prey, padding along on cushioned feet. Or they may lie hidden, waiting for the prey to pass. Suddenly the cat goes into action. It bounds forward and attacks. Its teeth are made for biting and cutting through flesh. Its feet are armed with sharp, hooked claws. (These are drawn into the paws when not needed.) A cat's are the sharpest claws of any meat-eating mammal. The cat kills and eats. Then it washes itself carefully.

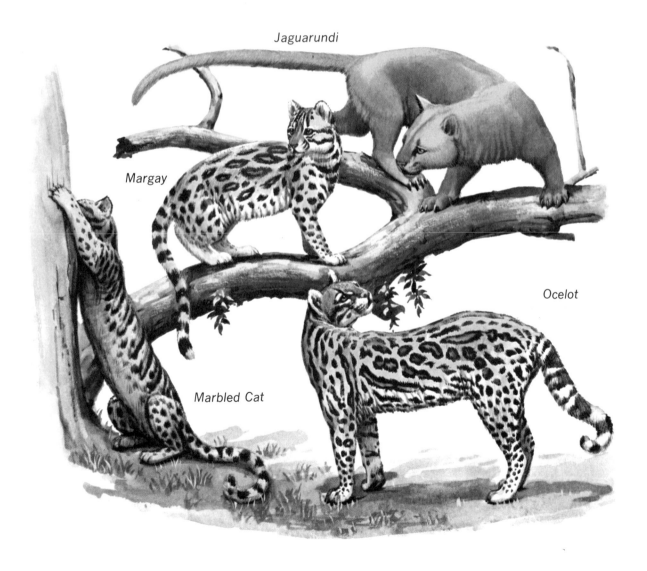

Jaguarundi

Margay

Marbled Cat

Ocelot

Like all hunting animals, cats are useful. Without the hunters, the earth would soon be overrun by rats, mice, rabbits, and hoofed mammals. Most kinds of cat hunt alone and live alone. Mothers stay with their young only until the young can hunt for themselves.

Scientists divide the cat family into two main groups. One group is made up of big cats—LIONS, TIGERS, LEOPARDS, and JAGUARS. All of them can roar. The other group is made up of smaller cats. None of them can really roar. MOUNTAIN LIONS, LYNXES, and CHEETAHS are three

such cats. Some of the others are shown in the drawings. Still other small cats live in South America, Africa, and Asia.

One of the small African cats is called the EGYPTIAN or KAFFIR CAT. Our house cats may be partly descended from this kind of cat. The ancient Egyptians tamed the Kaffir cat. From Egypt the cats spread to Europe. There they may have bred with European wildcats. In time the European house cats spread all over the world.

Today there are about nine kinds of DOMESTIC (tame) CAT. The best known

Pallas's Cat

Serval

Leopard Cat

23

Siamese Cat

Tabby

are the familiar short-haired house cats that do not belong to a breed. Then there are eight breeds of cat. Two are long-haired cats: the Persians and Himalayans. Six are short-haired cats: Abyssinians, Burmese, Manx, Russian Blue, Siamese, and Domestic Shorthair.

See also: CHEETAHS; JAGUARS; LEOPARDS; LIONS; LYNXES; MOUNTAIN LIONS; TIGERS

Persian

Cattle

In many parts of the world people raise cattle. Cattle are the familiar cows, bulls, calves, and steers that you see. A grown animal is 3 or 4 feet high at the shoulder and it weighs between 1,000 and 1,800 pounds.

Cattle eat mostly grass. When they are feeding, the grass goes into the first part of the stomach. Later when they are resting, they cough up the grass in mouthfuls. The mouthfuls are called the cud. The cattle chew the cud thoroughly and then swallow it. The cud goes on to the rest of the stomach. Cattle eat for about 8 hours out of the day. During this time a cow can eat some 155 pounds of green grass.

Cattle are raised for meat and milk. Parts of them are also used in making

Guernsey

products such as glue, soap, leather, fat, medicines, and fertilizers.

There are different breeds of cattle. Some give rich or large amounts of milk. The Jerseys, Guernseys, and Holsteins are famous for their milk. Other breeds are raised, for beef. The Hereford and Aberdeen Angus are two of these.

People have been raising cattle for at least 5,000 years. Most of today's breeds can be traced in part to a kind of wild cattle called the AUROCHS. The aurochs was once found in many parts of Europe, Asia, and North Africa. It died out 300 to 400 years ago.

In other parts of the world there are other kinds of cattle. Some are wild, and some are bred and raised by men. One of the best known is the YAK. It lives among the high plains and mountains of central Asia. Like all cattle, it has hooves and horns. It is a large, awkward-looking animal. But it climbs well. In Tibet yaks are raised for milk. They are also ridden, driven, and used as pack animals. The yak is sometimes called the grunting ox because of the noise it makes when it is overloaded.

Yak

Aberdeen Angus

Zebu

Holstein

Chamois

See Goats

Cheetahs

Cheetahs

Cheetahs are members of the cat family. But a cheetah is somewhat different from other cats. It has very long, slim legs. Its claws are like a dog's—they cannot be pulled back into the paw. They are always out. There is another way in which a cheetah is like a dog. It can be taught to hunt with men. In India cheetahs are trained to chase and bring down antelope.

Antelope are swift animals, but cheetahs are swifter still. They are the fastest of all land animals. They have been clocked at 70 miles an hour. A cheetah can keep up this pace for only 400 or 500 yards. But that is usually enough to let the cheetah catch its prey.

Cheetahs are found in eastern Africa and southern Asia. In the wild, they hunt by daylight and by moonlight. They hunt, catch, and eat antelope, birds, and small mammals such as hares. A mother cheetah has 2 to 4 young in a litter.

When tamed, cheetahs are likely to be gentle and loving.

Chimpanzees

A chimpanzee is one of the great apes. Like all true apes, it has no tail. Like all great apes, it is big and strong. But you can easily tell a chimpanzee from the other apes. All you have to do is look at the ears. If the ape has large ears that stick out from its head, it is a chimpanzee.

Chimpanzees live in the forests of Central Africa. They spend much of their time on the ground. Sometimes they walk on all fours—on their hind feet and the knuckles of their hands. Often they walk upright. By day the chimpanzees move about feeding. They eat mostly fruits, leaves, roots, and other plant matter. But they also catch insects and other small animals. At night each animal builds itself a shelter of branches. The shelter is used for only one night. The shelter may be built in a tree. Or it may be built on the ground in an area where there are no leopards.

Chimpanzees live in small groups. Mother chimpanzees spend their time taking care of their children. The children amuse themselves by climbing and by playing with other chimpanzees. They can touch a new baby. They can ride on the backs of males. They can invite themselves to dinner with another mother and child. Young chimpanzees do what they want to do, yet they are not spoiled. They never whine or whimper. They always obey their mothers. A mother carries her child around until it is about 4 years old. Children stay with their mothers until they are 8 or 9.

After man, chimpanzees are probably the most intelligent mammals. They enjoy change. They are full of curiosity about new things. They seem to puzzle over problems. They build shelters. They invent simple tools and weapons. They are quick to learn. A tame chimpanzee can learn many of the things that a 3-year-old child learns. In captivity some chimpanzees have lived 20 years. Under very good conditions they might live to be 30 or 40.

Chimpanzee

Chipmunks

Chipmunks are bright-eyed little animals that scurry about the woods and open fields. They have stripes on their backs, and they look very much like some of the striped ground squirrels. The best way to tell a chipmunk from a ground squirrel is by its cheeks. If the cheeks are striped, the animal is a chipmunk.

Chipmunks are found only in the Northern Hemisphere. About 17 kinds live in North America. The biggest is the EASTERN CHIPMUNK. It lives in south-eastern Canada and the eastern United States. Like other chipmunks, it will make friends with you, but it is a shy animal. If you startle it, it goes "chip, chip, chip," and then gives a sort of trill.

The eastern chipmunk can climb trees. But it would rather hunt its food on the ground. It eats seeds, grains, nuts, and berries. Some of the food is eaten at once. Some is gathered and stored for winter. A chipmunk has pouches inside its cheeks, where it can carry food. It

Eastern Chipmunk

darts about, stuffing seeds and nuts into its cheeks. Then it scampers home and unloads its cheek pouches.

Chipmunks live in burrows that they dig under logs or rocks. The burrow has a number of rooms. Some are for storing food. Some are for sleeping. Chipmunks are busy during the day and sleep at night. They also hibernate, or sleep away most of the winter. They wake up from time to time and eat some of the food they have stored. Then they go back to sleep. In spring a mother chipmunk gives birth to 3 to 5 babies.

The other American chipmunks are slightly smaller. They have more stripes and the coloring is slightly different. But their way of life is the same as the eastern chipmunk's.

Western Least Chipmunk

Conies
See Hyraxes; Pikas

Coons
See Raccoons

Cottontails
See Rabbits and Hares

Cougars
See Mountain Lions

The coyote is a member of the dog family. It looks something like a small German shepherd. And it is famous for its evening singing. Around twilight the coyote goes out to sing. It yaps, barks, whines, and howls. Sometimes coyotes also sing at dawn.

Coyotes live only in North America. They are found almost everywhere—from Alaska to Mexico, from the West Coast to the Adirondacks. They are much hunted, because they attack sheep. But they probably do more good than harm. They eat many mice, rats, and rabbits. They are intelligent animals and clever hunters. They seldom run as a pack. But they often hunt in pairs. One coyote chases the prey toward another, which lies hidden. Coyotes do not harm people.

Like wolves, many coyotes mate for life. Before the pups are born, the parents look for a den. It may be a cave, a hollow tree, or the burrow of some other animal. Here 6 to 7 pups are born. The mother stays with the pups and the father brings her food. Later both parents bring food to the pups. And still later the parents teach the pups to hunt.

Coyotes sometimes mate with dogs that live wild. The pups of these animals are called COY-DOGS.

Coyote

Deer

Deer are long-legged, graceful mammals. They live in almost every land area except Australia and Africa south of the Sahara. Deer are found in forests, deserts, swamps, open country, and the frozen lands of the far north.

There are more than 50 kinds of deer. Some kinds are as small as a fox terrier. Some are as big as a horse. Most are middle-sized.

Almost all kinds of male deer have antlers. A male uses his antlers as weapons. He uses them most during the mating season. Then the males often fight one another. Each is trying to gather as many females as possible. After the mating season the antlers are shed. Some of these rot away. Others are eaten by rodents such as porcupines, squirrels, and mice.

Antlers are made of bone. They grow from knobs on the deer's head. While they are growing, the antlers are covered with velvety skin. By late summer, the antlers are full grown. The velvety skin dries up. The deer rubs it off by scraping his antlers against trees and rocks.

Deer are prey for large meat-eating animals. Man also hunts them for their meat and hides. In some places there are no longer many big meat-eaters. Here deer may multiply so fast that there is not enough food for them. Unless there is some hunting of them, many will starve.

Deer are plant-eaters. They belong to the large group of hoofed mammals that chew their cud. When feeding, these mammals gulp down their food. Later they cough up mouthfuls of it and chew these thoroughly.

The WHITE-TAILED DEER is the most common kind in North America. There are several different races of white-tails. A northern one is the biggest, weighing about 300 pounds. The FLORIDA KEY DEER is the smallest; it weighs only 50 to 75 pounds. The white-tail lives in open woodlands. Its name comes from its tail, which is bright white on the underside. Fleeing an enemy, the deer holds its tail up. The flashing white serves as a warning of danger to other deer.

Like other deer, a mother white-tail has 1 or 2 fawns each spring. Baby fawns are weak and unsteady on their legs. They stay hidden, and their mother comes to feed them. She warns them to stay quietly on the ground. The fawns do not begin to follow their mother until they are about 4 weeks old. A fawn's coat is covered with white spots. These help to hide it in the sun and shadows of the woods.

Two other common deer are the MULE DEER and the BLACK-TAILED DEER. They are found in western North America. A mule deer has very large ears. The black-tail is famous for its bounding leaps. It is

Whitetail Deer and fawn

a very fast runner.

The American ELK is a much bigger deer. A male may stand 5 feet tall at the shoulder and weigh up to 600 pounds. Elk live in parts of Canada and the western United States. They move around in herds, feeding on grass and other plants. Elk are sometimes called by their Indian name, which is WAPITI. They are closely related to the RED DEER of Europe. Two other large deer are the MOOSE and the REINDEER.

See also: MOOSE; REINDEER

Caribou

Elk

Black-Tailed Deer

Mule Deer

Moose

31

Dogs

Almost anywhere that you find people you will find dogs. Some are working dogs. They pull sleds, herd sheep, stand guard, or help men hunt. Others are kept as pets. In the United States alone, there are some 26 million pet dogs and working dogs. Some are breeds. Some are a mixture of breeds. All of them are called "domestic dogs." That means they are tame dogs that live with people.

There are also many kinds of wild dog in the world. WOLVES, FOXES, COYOTES, and JACKALS are just a few of the wild dogs. Wild dogs are found in all parts of the world except Antarctica. The largest are the ARCTIC WOLVES.

All wild dogs are meat-eaters. They catch and kill other animals for food. Their senses of sight, smell, and hearing are keen. They have long legs and are good runners. Most kinds of wild dog hunt in packs. They may chase their prey for hours. Then they attack. The wild dogs gobble their dinner, stuffing until they can eat no more. If some food is left over, they may bury or hide it to eat later.

A wild dog usually has a thick coat of fur, a bushy tail, and pointed ears. At the end of each toe there is a strong claw. A dog's claws are always out. They cannot be drawn back into the paw as a cat's can. The muzzle is broad at the jaws and slender at the nose. Like a domestic dog, the wild dog pants when it is hot. A dog sweats only on the tongue.

The wild dogs are intelligent and brave. They are also social animals. This means that they live together in groups. Some kinds seem to mate for life. And a father usually helps to take care of the young.

Some of the wild dogs are well-known.

Dhole

Cape Hunting Dog

Maned Wolf

Bush Dog

Raccoon Dog

Yodeling Dog

Dingo

German Shepherd

Others are little-known. The drawings show some of the little-known wild dogs. One wild dog presents something of a mystery. This is the DINGO, which lives in Australia. Scientists do not think it is native to Australia. But they do not know where it came from. Probably the first tribesmen to reach Australia brought the dingo with them. Perhaps they used it for hunting. As time passed, some dingos ran wild. Others stayed with the tribes. To-day's tribesmen keep dingos as pets and as hunting dogs. Only one thing seems fairly sure. The dingo must once have been a wild dog that very early people tamed.

Fox Terrier

Basset

Dalmatian

33

In fact, that is how all our domestic dogs came into being. In the beginning, early man probably feared and hated the wild dogs. The dogs hung around his camp and stole his meat. They hunted the same animals that he did. And so the dogs were enemies. But sometimes a hunter came on a litter of pups. The pups were playful balls of fur. The hunter took them home to his own children. The pups grew up tame. And people began to discover that tame dogs could be useful. They gave warning of danger. They drove other animals away from the camps. They helped in the hunting. The long friend-ship between dogs and people had begun.

When tribes of people moved around, they met other tribes with other kinds of dogs. The different dogs mated. And pups that were born were not quite like any of the wild dogs. They were a new sort of dog.

In time people learned to breed the sorts of dogs that they wanted. They bred dogs that could run fast or swim well or go after a burrowing animal. In this way different breeds of dog developed. Today there are about 200 breeds in the world. *See also:* COYOTES; FOXES; JACKALS; WOLVES

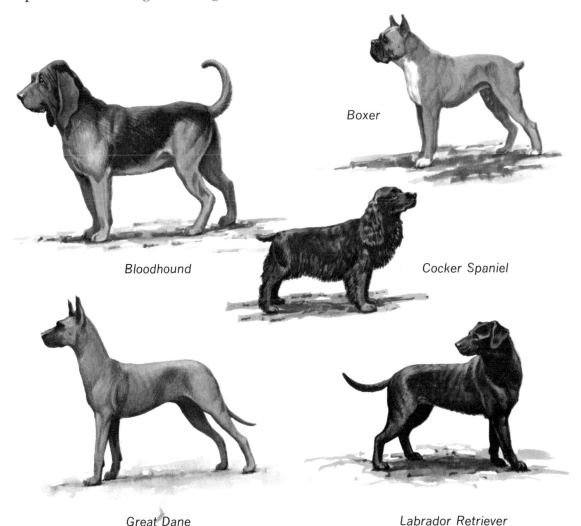

Boxer

Bloodhound

Cocker Spaniel

Great Dane

Labrador Retriever

34

Dolphins

Dolphins are mammals that live in the sea. A dolphin is born in the sea. It plays, feeds, and sleeps in the sea. It spends its whole life in the sea, for it cannot live on land.

A dolphin swims by moving its powerful tail up and down. And it is an excellent swimmer. Dolphins enjoy playing around ships and riding the bow waves. They can easily keep up with a ship traveling at 25 miles an hour. A dolphin can stay underwater for 4 to 6 minutes. Then it must surface for air. It breathes through its nostrils. These are on the top of its head and are called the blowhole. A cover over the blowhole snaps shut when the dolphin dives.

Many dolphins live along coasts and sometimes swim into bays and the mouths of rivers. Here they can swim at top speed, finding their way in muddy water and at night. They can also find and catch fish, which is what dolphins eat. For a long time scientists did not understand how dolphins could do all this. Then they discovered the answer. A dolphin makes many kinds of noises. One is a clicking sound. A swimming dolphin sends out bursts of clicks. These sounds travel through the water. When they hit a solid object, they bounce off it. The dolphin hears the echoes. The echoes tell the dolphin what lies ahead. That is how it finds food. That is how it avoids hitting things.

A baby dolphin is born tail-first underwater. Its mother pushes it to the surface for its first breath of air. But it is born able to see and to swim. It nurses underwater on milk. At the time it is born, it has a few bristles on its snout. These later fall out. A full-grown dolphin has no hair. A mother dolphin takes very good care of her baby. She is helped by a friend, who acts as the baby's aunt. In fact, dolphins often help one another. If one dolphin is hurt or sick, two others will help to hold it up in the water so that it can breathe.

Another nice thing about dolphins is

Dolphin

Porpoise

that they like people. Dolphins have long made friends with swimmers and fishermen. Most often they have made friends with children. They have played with children in the water and even taken them for rides.

Many dolphins have been kept in aquariums. Perhaps you have seen them there or on TV. Young dolphins are very playful. They make up their own games. Sometimes they play with one another. Sometimes a dolphin teaches its game to people. Dolphins are very intelligent. Scientists say they are certainly as intelligent as dogs. They may be even more intelligent.

There are many kinds of dolphin in the world. All are members of the whale family. They belong to the branch called toothed whales. They are fairly small—between 5 and 14 feet long. Their closest relatives are the PORPOISES. Dolphins and porpoises are very much alike. They are so much alike that it is hard to tell them apart. Most people call them all by one name—either dolphins or porpoises.

Donkeys

A donkey is a small, long-eared member of the horse family. It is sturdily built. It is sure-footed. And it is hardy. A donkey works well in hot climates. It needs less water than a horse. And it can live on weeds and other foods that would not keep a horse alive. Donkeys can live and work in many places where horses cannot. Donkeys are used for riding and as beasts of burden. They are also used as pack animals in rocky or steep areas. The sure-footed donkey can pick its way safely over ground where a horse might slip and fall.

Pack Donkey

Mule

Hinny

Donkeys have been used by men for thousands of years. They are descended from the wild asses of northern Africa. "Donkey" is simply another name for ass. Usually it means a tamed ass.

Sometimes donkeys and horses mate. If the father is a donkey, the young animal is called a MULE. If the father is a horse, the young animal is called a HINNY. Mules are bigger and stronger than hinnies. Neither mules nor hinnies are able to have young of their own.

Duckbills
See Platypuses

Dugongs
See Sea Cows

Elephants

Once you have seen an elephant, you can never forget it. To begin with, an elephant is very big. It is the biggest land mammal alive. It stands 10 or 11 feet high at the shoulder and may weigh 5 or 6 tons. This mountain of a mammal is clothed in a wrinkled, gray hide. It has legs like pillars and ears like huge fans. Small eyes with long lashes look out at the world from a huge head. And then there is the trunk, which is really the elephant's nose. No other mammal has such a nose —or such a useful nose.

An elephant uses its trunk for eating. It gathers food with its trunk and then stuffs the food into its mouth. Elephants eat plant food. In the wild, an elephant strips branches off trees, pulls up grass, and picks fruit. A big male may eat 300 to 500 pounds of food a day.

An elephant uses its trunk for drinking. It sucks water into the trunk. Then it blows the water into its mouth. It may drink 50 gallons of water a day.

An elephant washes with its trunk. It sucks water into the trunk and then sprays its back. It smells with its trunk. That is how it learns what is going on, for it does not have keen eyes. It tests the ground with its trunk. It examines strange objects with its trunk.

The trunk is used for lifting things. An elephant can pick up a tree trunk that weighs nearly a ton. It can pick up a pea-

37

nut from the floor. If you look closely at the end of the trunk, you will see a fleshy "finger" there. That is what the elephant uses when it picks up something very small.

The trunk is also used for affection. Elephants pat each other when courting. A mother fondles her baby with her trunk.

In the wild, elephants live in herds of 10 to 50 animals. They eat a great deal. So they must travel far and wide to find food. They are good swimmers and often cross large rivers. In fact, the herd is never far from water. In early morning the elephants drink and bathe, rolling and splashing in the water. Then they feed for several hours. Around noon the herd rests in the shade. Later it goes back to a river or lake and then feeds again. At night some elephants lie down to sleep. But most sleep standing up.

A newborn elephant is a big baby. It is 3 feet high at the shoulder and may weigh 300 pounds. It is also covered with hair. Most of this hair later falls out. A grown elephant has only bristles on its hide. A baby is able to walk an hour or two after it is born. It travels with the herd. It nurses for about 2 years and stays with its mother until it is at least 4. Elephants live a long time. They may live to be 60 or 70.

Most of the elephants in circuses are ASIATIC ELEPHANTS. They come from

Asiatic Elephant

African Elephant

India, Ceylon, and Southeast Asia. Sometimes they are called INDIAN ELEPHANTS. Another kind of elephant lives in Africa, south of the Sahara. It is called the AFRICAN ELEPHANT. Many zoos have both kinds.

African and Asian elephants look much alike. But you can tell them apart if you know what to look for. An African elephant has two fingers at the tip of its trunk. Its ears are huge. The Asiatic elephant has one finger at the tip of the trunk. Its ears are smaller.

Elephants are intelligent, strong, and fairly easy to tame. Men have been putting them to work for hundreds of years. In India and Burma they have long been used for many purposes. They are taught to pick up and carry heavy logs. People ride them when hunting tigers.

African Elephants bathing

Elk

See Deer

Ermines

See Weasels

American Gray Fox

Fennec Fox

There are many other kinds of fox. The AMERICAN GRAY FOX can sometimes climb for a few feet into slanting trees. It hugs the trunk with its front legs and pushes itself up with its hind legs. The KIT FOXES and SWIFT FOXES are the smallest ones in North America. They weigh 4 to 5 pounds. The kit fox lives on western plains. The swift fox lives on deserts of the Southwest.

Other kinds of foxes live in other parts of the world. Perhaps the most beautiful one is the FENNEC FOX. It lives in desert areas of northern Africa. It is also the smallest member of the wild dog family. About 16 inches long, it weighs 2 to 4 pounds.

Gibbons

See Apes

Giraffes

A giraffe is the tallest animal in the world. The head of a big male is 18 or 19 feet above the ground. He may weigh more than 2 tons.

This giant animal eats mostly leaves and grass. A giraffe reaches into the branches of a tree. It wraps its very long tongue around some leaves and pulls them into its mouth. Then it nibbles them off. Eating grass is a very different matter. A giraffe has a long neck, but it also has long legs. To eat grass or drink water, it must spread its front legs apart. Only then can its head reach the ground.

Giraffes live in Africa. They are usually seen on dry, sunny plains and along the edges of forests. They move about in

Giraffe

Giraffes

small herds. They are always alert for danger. Their keen eyes and great height give them a good view of the land. If they are alarmed, their long legs carry them off at speeds up to 30 miles an hour. Lions are their chief enemies. If attacked, a giraffe defends itself with its big front hooves.

Both male and female giraffes have horns. The horns are made of bone, and they are covered with skin and hair. When males fight, they butt each other with their heads and necks. Males fight during the mating season. A mother giraffe bears a single baby. At birth the baby is about $6\frac{1}{2}$ feet tall. Young giraffes usually lie down to sleep. But most grown giraffes sleep standing up.

The giraffe has a short-necked relative called the OKAPI. The okapi lives in rain forests of central Africa. It is a shy animal, about the size of a horse. A male has short, hair-covered horns.

Okapi

43

Goats

Domestic Goat

Ibex

About 8,000 or 9,000 years ago men first began to raise goats. The goats were wild animals that early farmers started to keep in herds. Today there are many breeds of goat. They are raised for meat and for milk, which can be made into butter and cheese. They are raised for hides and for hair. Like the wool of sheep, goat hair can be made into clothing. Cashmere, mohair, and angora are fine wools that are made from goat hairs.

Several kinds of wild goat still live in the Northern Hemisphere. Like wild sheep, they live in rugged mountain country. And they look very much like wild sheep. It is often hard to tell which you are looking at. The best clue is a beard. Male goats have beards. Male sheep do not. The IBEX is one of the best-known Old World goats.

North America has an animal called the ROCKY MOUNTAIN GOAT. It is not a true goat, but is a goat-antelope. Its horns are smaller than a true goat's. Its neck and shoulders are heavier.

The Rocky Mountain goat is found from southern Alaska to northern Idaho. It is slow-moving. But it climbs with sure-footed ease in the steep, rocky places where it lives. Its hooves have a hard,

Chamois

Rocky Mountain Goat

sharp rim. Within the rim is a soft, inner pad. Such feet grip the surface of rocks and ice. The goat feeds on woody plants and may graze on grass.

Kids are born in the spring. One or two are born to a mother each year. Half an hour after its birth, a kid is able to jump about. But the mother keeps it hidden for a few days. She goes off to feed and comes back to nurse the kid. In a few days they join a band of other mothers and their young. The mothers guard their young until the kids are big enough to take care of themselves.

The Rocky Mountain goat is closely related to the CHAMOIS of Europe and Asia Minor. The chamois is a small mammal that lives among high mountain peaks. It is nimble, daring, and graceful. Alarmed, a band of chamois take off in flight. They skim over the mountainside, jumping from one narrow ledge to another.

Gophers

See Pocket Gophers; Squirrels

Gorillas

Gorillas

Gorillas are the biggest of the great apes. And they are very big indeed. A male stands about $5\frac{1}{2}$ feet tall. He weighs between 300 and 500 pounds. A growling, angry gorilla is a frightening animal. Almost no other animal will attack it. But usually a gorilla is quiet and shy. It is dangerous only when attacked or threatened.

Gorillas feed mostly on juicy-stemmed plants. But they also eat fruits, leaves, berries, and buds. All climb trees to get food. Females and their young may travel through the trees. Males seldom do. Their great weight makes tree travel dangerous.

On the ground, males often stand upright. But they usually walk on all fours—on their hind feet and the knuckles of their hands.

At night the females build shelters in trees. A male is more likely to build a shelter at the foot of a tree.

Gorillas live in the forests of Central Africa. One kind lives in the lowlands. Another kind lives in mountain forests. There are not many gorillas left today— perhaps about 10,000. They are hunted by natives for their meat and skins. The gorillas you see in zoos and circuses were probably captured as babies.

Grizzly Bears
See Bears

Groundhogs
See Woodchucks

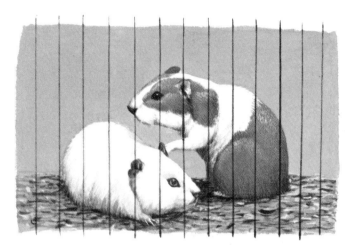

Guinea Pigs

The guinea pig is a native of South America. In spite of its name, it is not a pig. It is one of the rodents, or gnawing mammals. It is a small animal with a plump body, short legs, and no tail. In the wild, guinea pigs live together in burrows. They are shy animals, always ready to take alarm and run. They eat leaves, grain, and other plant food. The Inca Indians of Peru used to raise guinea pigs and eat them.

Today guinea pigs are raised in laboratories all over the world. Scientists use them to study disease and diet and to show how traits are passed down through families. Guinea pigs are good to use in such studies because they breed quickly and often. A mother guinea pig has litters of 3 or 4 young. She may have 5 or 6 litters a year. Each of the young is ready to start breeding at the age of 2 months. Guinea pigs live to be about 8 years old.

Guinea pigs are gentle and do not bite. They are easy to raise if they are fed and kept warm and clean.

Hamsters

A hamster is a small, chubby animal. It has short legs, a stub of a tail, and thick, soft fur. It is a rodent, or gnawing mammal. There are three main types of hamster. All are natives of the Old World. The ones you see in pet shops and zoos are usually golden hamsters. They are native to Syria.

A GOLDEN HAMSTER has huge pouches inside its cheeks. They reach from the lips to the shoulders. A hamster uses the pouches to carry food back to its burrow. When the pouches are filled, the hamster's head and shoulders look very fat. These hamsters eat almost everything— green plants, seeds, fruits, and meat. Like many small creatures, they are most active at night. A mother hamster usually has a litter of 6 or 7 young. She bears several litters a year. A hamster lives to be 2 or 3 years old.

Hamster

Hares

See Rabbits and Hares

47

Hedgehogs

Hedgehog

A European hedgehog is a small, plump animal about $5\frac{1}{4}$ to 10 inches long. By day it sleeps in the burrow it has dug under a hedge or bush. At night it comes out and searches for food. Many meat-eating animals think a hedgehog would make a tasty meal. But they seldom get a chance to find out, for a hedgehog is a walking pincushion. At the first sign of danger, it rolls itself into a ball. Its furry head, legs, and underside are safely tucked away. An enemy is faced with a ball of needle-sharp quills.

When the enemy goes away, the hedgehog uncurls. It goes on about its business of hunting food. It likes insects best. But it also eats frogs, snails, snakes, young birds, and mice. Sometimes it eats fruits and other vegetable matter. In autumn the hedgehog grows very fat. Its body draws on this fat while the hedge-

Hedgehog quill

hog sleeps away the coldest part of the winter.

Once or twice a year a mother hedgehog has a litter of 5 to 7 young. The young are born with quills, but the quills are soft. They harden within a few weeks. The quills are a form of hair.

There are several kinds of hedgehog. All are found only in the Old World. They are not the same as porcupines. A porcupine is a rodent or gnawing mammal. A hedgehog belongs to the same family as the moles and shrews.

48

Hippopotamuses

The common hippopotamus has a 4-ton body on short, thick legs. The great body just clears the ground. Small, bulging eyes look out of the huge head. While you watch a hippo at the zoo, it may yawn. The vast, pink mouth opens wide, and you see the animal's tusks. Perhaps the hippo will then decide to take a swim. It lumbers over to its pool and slides into the water. It may stay underwater for a few minutes. Then it may float, with only its eyes and nostrils showing above the water. You see that the bulging eyes and nostrils are useful.

In Africa, where they live, hippos spend much of their time in water. Sometimes they wade about, snorting and bellowing and rooting up food. Sometimes they paddle or float or sink to the bottom. A hippo can stay underwater for as long as half an hour. It is also able to walk about on the bottom of a river or lake.

In many ways, hippos are water animals. A baby hippo is born underwater and nurses underwater. Until it learns to swim, the mother may carry it on her back. A hippo needs to stay moist. Its hide has special pores. They give off a thick, oily, pink stuff called "blood sweat." This thick stuff protects the hide and keeps it from drying out on land.

Common hippos spend the day dozing in or near water. At night they roam about looking for food. They eat mostly grass, but sometimes they raid a farmer's fields. Hippos are much hunted by natives for their flesh and hides. Their tusks are excellent ivory.

A much smaller hippo lives in the forests and swamps of West Africa. It is the PIGMY HIPPOPOTAMUS. This hippo spends much more time on land than the common hippo does.

Hippopotamuses

Hogs

See Pigs

Horses

A fine horse is an intelligent and handsome animal. The graceful body is designed for speed. It is designed for running on hard ground. It is designed for escaping enemies in a burst of speed.

The running muscles are bunched at the tops of the legs. The legs themselves are long and slender. Each ends in a single toe, which is covered by a hard hoof. A horse is always poised on the tips of its toes, ready for flight.

A horse's eyes are set well back on the head. The horse can see all around itself. It can see backward as well as forward, without turning its head. When it puts its long neck and head down, it can easily reach the grass that is its food. At the same time it sees what is happening around it. And it stands ready to run if danger threatens.

A horse looks alert, and it is. Its eyesight is keen. So are its senses of smelling and hearing. The ears twitch, picking up faint sounds. The nostrils gulp in large amounts of air.

Through the ages, their keen senses and long legs have helped horses escape most of their meat-eating enemies.

The horse itself is a plant-eater. It eats mostly coarse grasses. It cuts off a mouthful with its front teeth. It grinds the grass with its back teeth. Grass wears teeth down. That is one reason why an expert can tell the age of a horse by looking at its teeth. Horses are old at 20, but some live to be 30 or 40.

Men first began to capture and tame wild horses about 5,000 years ago. Since then, they have developed many different breeds. Some have been bred for large size. Big and strong, these horses are used for plowing, for pulling loads, and for other heavy work. Some horses are slender and streamlined. They are used for riding, racing, and hunting.

All told, there are about 60 breeds of horse today. The biggest is probably the SHIRE HORSE. This powerful workhorse is nearly 6 feet high at the shoulder and may weigh 2,200 to 2,400 pounds. The smallest is the SHETLAND PONY. (A pony is simply a small horse.) Many Shetlands are less than 3 feet high at the shoulder. They are, however, very strong and hardy.

There are very few true wild horses in the world today. In many places there are herds of horses that live in the wild. But these are horses that men have bred. They have either escaped or been turned loose. This is true of the "wild horses" of the western United States. They are descended from horses that the Spaniards brought to the New World. They are called MUSTANGS, from the Spanish word that means "strayed" or "wild."

Mustang

Przewalski's Horse

Shire

Shetland Pony

Thoroughbred

Pinto

In the early 1800's more than a million mustangs ranged the western plains and deserts. Settlers captured and tamed many of the mustangs. Later, ranchers took over the land for cattle. Today only a few hundred mustangs are left.

The mustangs live together in small bands. A band usually roams one area where there is food and water. The band is made up of mares and their young, and it is led by a stallion. Each stallion gathers as many mares as he can for his own band. He may try to steal mares from another band. If he does, a fight takes place. The two stallions scream and rear on their hind legs. They strike with their front hooves and bite with their teeth. The winner takes as many mares as he can and goes on his way. Colts, or foals, are born in spring. Usually a mare has one colt every other year. The young stay with their mothers for about a year. Then the stallion drives them out of the band.

The MONGOLIAN WILD HORSES may be truly wild. Slightly larger than a pony, this horse has a flowing tail and a short mane. It is also called PRZEWALSKI's HORSE after the Russian explorer who discovered it. No one is sure whether these horses are still of pure stock. They may have bred with other horses that live in the wild. Only a few of them still run wild.

Horses have several close relatives. The best known is the ZEBRA. Another is the WILD ASS of northern and eastern Africa. Still others are the asslike animals of Asia.

See also: DONKEYS; ZEBRAS

Arabian Horse

Hyenas

Spotted Hyena

The SPOTTED HYENA is often called the LAUGHING HYENA. It does not really laugh. But it howls, gurgles, and makes a strange cackling noise when it is excited. This hyena is about 3 feet high at the shoulder and may weigh 175 pounds. It looks awkward because its front legs are longer than its hind legs. But it is a swift animal. It can run as fast as 35 or 40 miles an hour.

The spotted hyena lives in a burrow or cave. It sleeps by day. At night it comes out to eat. Like all hyenas, it is a meat-eater with big, strong jaws. It hunts as part of a pack.

People long thought that hyenas were cowards. They were thought to eat mostly what other hunters, such as lions, had left.

New studies show this may not be true. Some, and perhaps all, hyenas are very brave. They attack even large, fierce animals, such as African buffaloes. When the kill is made, the hyenas bark, growl, and shriek. The lions hear the noise and come running. Then there is another fight. If the lions win, they get the meat and the hyenas get the leftovers. If the hyenas win, they get the meat.

There are three kinds of hyena—the spotted, the striped, and the brown hyena. All are found in parts of Africa. The STRIPED HYENA is also found as far east as India. Hyenas look something like ugly dogs. But they are not members of the dog family. They form a separate family of their own.

Striped Hyena

Hyraxes

Rock Hyrax

A hyrax looks somewhat like a rabbit with small ears and short legs. Its toes have flat nails that look like hooves. The soles of the feet are padded and damp. The middle of the sole can be pulled up. This forms a cup that sucks at the surface. A hyrax can stick to almost any surface. It never skids. Hyraxes can climb trees. And they are very good at running over rocks and about cliffs.

There are several kinds of hyrax. All live in the Old World—in Africa and the Middle East. They are sometimes called DASSIES. In the Bible they are called CONIES.

Three kinds of hyrax live in trees. They spend the day in tree hollows or hidden among the leaves. At night they run up and down trees, feeding on leaves, buds, and insects. They are known for the noise they make. It starts as a croaking sound. The croaking becomes louder and louder and ends in a scream.

Six kinds of hyrax live on the ground. They are active by day. They enjoy basking in the sun and rolling in dust. They like to chase one another among the rocks. They are small animals that eat locusts, roots, and bulbs. But they will bite any animal that bothers them. These hyraxes live together in large colonies. They are very noisy, too. They whistle, scream, and chatter. A mother usually has a litter of 3 young. A few hours after birth they are able to run around with the other hyraxes.

Jackals

Jackals belong to the big family of wild dogs. They are Old World animals that live in warm, fairly dry areas. There are several kinds of jackal. But all have the same way of life.

Jackals will eat almost anything—mice, rats, chickens, lambs, goats, lizards, insects, grapes, and sugar cane. They are best known for eating what is left by lions and tigers. When it scents a kill, a jackal goes to the place where the lion or tiger is eating. It sits down and waits.

55

When the big cat has eaten its fill, the jackal feasts on the remains.

Jackals are stealthy animals. They are seldom seen by people. In areas where people live, the jackal comes out only at night. Then it hunts in family groups or in small packs. When not hunting, a jackal stays by itself.

Like the American coyote, the jackal "sings" in the evening. At sundown it goes out and howls. It gives three or four long wails and then some short yelps.

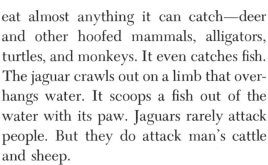

Jackal

Jack Rabbits *See Rabbits and Hares*

Jaguars

In a zoo it is hard to tell a jaguar from a leopard. They are both big cats. And both have yellow-tan coats with black spots. In the wild you cannot mistake them. Jaguars are found only in the New World, while leopards are found only in the Old World. Jaguars live in many parts of South America and as far north as Mexico. They are the biggest of the New World cats. A male may weigh as much as 250 pounds.

A jaguar likes best to live in a jungle. But it can also live in deserts and on open plains. It is a good climber and swimmer, but it hunts mostly on the ground. It will eat almost anything it can catch—deer and other hoofed mammals, alligators, turtles, and monkeys. It even catches fish. The jaguar crawls out on a limb that overhangs water. It scoops a fish out of the water with its paw. Jaguars rarely attack people. But they do attack man's cattle and sheep.

Young jaguars are born in a den. There may be 2 to 4 of them in a litter. They stay with their mother for about 2 years. Then they are ready to hunt and earn their own living.

Jaguar

Kangaroos

Great Gray Kangaroo

In the cool of early morning the great gray kangaroos feed on grass. The sun rises and the day becomes hot. The great grays rest in the tall grass. They wash themselves. From time to time they rise to scratch themselves or look about. Perhaps one sees something moving—an eagle circling overhead. It gives an alarm thump of its feet. Instantly the others are up and moving. They bound away on their big hind legs.

Hopping slowly, a kangaroo bounces along on its hind legs. It may lazily thump the ground with its tail. Hopping faster, the kangaroo carries its tail in the air. The tail helps to balance the kangaroo and also serves as a rudder. A big kangaroo covers about 25 feet in each leap. It can easily speed along at 20 miles an hour.

The great gray is a big kangaroo. When a male rears up, he can look over a man's head. He may weigh as much as 200 pounds.

A female is smaller and slimmer. Like all kangaroo mothers, she carries her baby in a pouch on her stomach. At birth the baby of a great gray is less than an inch long. All by itself this tiny baby crawls through its mother's fur and scrambles into her pouch. There it clamps onto a nipple and begins to feed. It first leaves the pouch when it is about 4 months old. It tries out its legs and samples some grass. By the time it is 8 months old, it has outgrown the pouch.

Kangaroos belong to the big group of

animals called marsupials, or pouched mammals. Almost all these mammals live in Australia and on neighboring islands. There are many types of marsupial. Kangaroos are just one type—and there are 45 to 50 kinds of kangaroo. They are of many sizes.

The heaviest is the GREAT GRAY, or FORESTER, KANGAROO. The RED KANGAROO is taller but more slender. The male is wine-red in color. The female is a soft, smoky-blue.

Red Kangaroo

The smallest kangaroos are only a foot high. They belong to the group called RAT KANGAROOS. Rat kangaroos make nests of grass. They stay in their nests by day and come out at night.

Other kangaroos are small, medium, and large in size. The different kinds are found in all sorts of places—deserts, swamps, woods, rocks, and cliffs. One kind, the TREE KANGAROO, lives in trees. It is a splendid climber and acrobat.

Tree Kangaroo

Koalas

Koala

A koala has a woolly coat, a black snub nose, and round bushy ears. Its eyes are small and bright. A full-grown koala is $2\frac{1}{2}$ to 3 feet long and weighs about 30 pounds. It is a gentle, quiet animal that never does any harm.

The koala looks like a teddy bear, but it is not a bear. It is one of the mammals that carry their young in pouches. Koalas are found only in Australia. They are very good at climbing trees. They eat the leaves of eucalyptus trees, which are also called gum trees. A koala eats about 2 pounds of leaves a day. It is not a water-drinker. It gets its water from dew on the leaves and from the leaves themselves.

A mother koala usually has a baby every other year. At birth the baby is less than an inch long. It climbs into its mother's pouch and attaches itself to a nipple. When it grows too big for the pouch, it comes out. It then travels on its mother's back until it is almost as big as she is. When the baby is cold or resting, the mother hugs it in her lap.

Lemmings

A lemming is like a chubby field mouse with a very short tail. There are four kinds of lemming. All live in the far north of the world. In winter they tunnel under the snow. In summer they live on the surface of the ground or burrow through the soil. They eat grasses, leaves, berries, blossoms, and roots. Female lemmings make nests of grass, moss, and lichens. Several litters of 3 to 9 young are born in a nest each year.

Norway lemmings are famous for the journeys that they make. This is what happens. When there is lots of food, lemmings multiply very quickly. These many, many lemmings gobble up the food. Soon there is little left to eat. Then thousands

upon thousands of lemmings set out to find food. Huge bands of them swarm across the land. They travel through swamps, cities, and forests. They swim rivers and lakes. Many die along the way. But many others finally reach the sea. To

Lemming

them the sea is simply more water to cross. Thousands of them plunge in. They swim until they drown.

By this time there are not many lemmings left at home. There is enough food for them. So again the lemmings multiply. And in 3 or 4 years another journey to the sea takes place.

Many other animals are affected by what happens to the lemmings. Lemmings eat the same food as caribou and reindeer. When there are many lemmings, the caribou and reindeer may starve. Lemmings themselves are eaten by many mammals and birds. When there are few lemmings, the animals that prey on them must move south to find food.

Leopards

A leopard is smaller than a lion or a tiger. But it is still one of the big cats. It is about 7 feet long from its nose to the end of its tail. It weighs from 100 to 175 pounds. A leopard is intelligent. It is quick to learn, and it remembers what it has learned. It is a fierce fighter and a dangerous animal.

A leopard is a good climber. It hides among the branches of a tree, waiting for another animal to pass. The leopard leaps on its prey and kills. It may drag its food back into the tree and eat there. On the ground a leopard springs after its prey. It may catch the other animal in a few long leaps. Leopards prey on deer, antelope, monkeys, cattle, sheep, and small animals. They usually hunt alone.

Leopard are found mainly in Africa and Asia. There may still be a few in southeastern Europe.

Most leopards have a bright yellow coat with black spots. You may hear of an animal called a BLACK PANTHER. This is really a leopard that happens to be black. A black leopard can be born in the same litter with spotted leopard cubs. A mother leopard has a litter of 1 to 4 young. They are full grown at the age of 3 years. In a zoo a leopard may live to be 20.

Leopards

Lions

The lion is often called the king of the beasts. He has a thundering roar. He has a mane of long hair on his head and shoulders. And he is a big animal. He stands 3 feet high at the shoulder. He may weigh as much as 500 pounds. (A lioness is smaller and does not have a mane.)

Lions are hunters and meat-eaters. They live in open country and on grassy plains. They hunt hoofed mammals that also live in such areas. Zebras and antelope are their favorite prey. Lions also eat some smaller mammals.

Like the rest of the cat family, lions hunt chiefly at night. A lion pads quietly along on cushioned feet. It can run in spurts of 40 miles an hour. Its powerful muscles carry it through the air in long leaps. A lion attacks with claws and teeth.

Unlike other cats, lions enjoy company. They live together in groups called prides. A pride is a family-sized group. It is made up of several females, one or more males, and a number of young lions. Sometimes the lions hunt together. A male drives the prey to where his mate lies in wait.

When a big kill is made, the lions eat from it for several days. When the food is used up, they kill again. Lions kill only for food or to defend themselves.

A mother lion usually has a litter of about 4 cubs. Unlike other cats, the lion is a good father. He brings food to the lioness. Later he may bring food for the whole family. Young lions do not start to hunt for their own food until they are a year old.

Most lions live in Africa, south of the Sahara. There are also a few lions in northwest India.

Lions are often seen in circuses. They are intelligent animals. They are more friendly than other big cats. So it is fairly easy to teach them tricks. But a lion is never truly tamed. The trainer must always be on guard.

Llamas

Llama

Guanaco

Llamas are members of the camel family. They live in the Andes Mountains of South America. Llamas were first tamed and put to work by the Inca Indians about 2,500 years ago. The llama is much used as a beast of burden. It can carry loads of 200 pounds over the rugged mountains. But like the camel, the llama is a strong-willed animal. If overloaded, it sits down and will not move. If made angry, it spits on the person who annoyed it.

Today's Indians use almost every part of a llama. They eat its meat. They weave its fleece into cloth and make sandals from its hide. They make candles from its fat and braid rope from its long hairs. Llama droppings serve as fuel in a tree-less land.

Llamas may be a tamed form of the GUANACO. This wild animal still lives in small herds in the Andes. Guanacos are alert animals that depend on speed for safety. They can run at speeds of up to 35 miles an hour. They eat grass and en-joy bathing in mountain streams. A baby guanaco is able to run as soon as it is born.

Alpaca

The ALPACA may be another tamed form of the guanaco. An alpaca looks like a llama with very long hair. Its woolly coat hangs over its eyes, and the wool of its body may drag on the ground. The alpaca is raised for its wool, which is woven into a very fine cloth.

The VICUÑA is related to the guanaco family. It looks something like a guanaco but is smaller and more slender. Small herds of vicuñas are found high in the Andes. Their silky fleece is highly prized as wool.

Vicuña

Lynxes

Lynxes are cats. But they look rather different from other cats. A lynx has long side whiskers. It has tufts of fur at the tips of its ears. It has a short tail and large feet. Its hind legs are longer than its front legs.

There are several kinds of lynx. Two kinds live in North America. One is the CANADA LYNX. The other is the BOBCAT, which is also called the BAY LYNX or WILDCAT.

Most Canada lynxes live in Alaska and Canada, but some cross the border into Oregon, Colorado, and northern New York. The Canada lynx hunts at night. Its favorite food is the snowshoe hare. This lynx weighs between 20 and 40 pounds. When the ground is covered with snow, its big feet act as snowshoes. It is good at climbing and swimming. A mother has litters of 1 to 4 young.

The bobcat is smaller than the Canada

Canada Lynx

The FIELD MOUSE is another familiar mouse. It is also called a MEADOW MOUSE or a VOLE. Several kinds of field mice are native to the New World. The common field mouse looks like a house mouse with a short tail.

Field mice are food for almost all meat-eating mammals, birds, snakes, and turtles. Few field mice live to be a year old. But like house mice, they breed very, very quickly. The young are born in a round nest of dry plant material.

Common Field Mouse

The many kinds of field mice eat mostly seeds, plants, and insects. Where there are many field mice, they do great damage to crops.

North America has many other kinds of native mice. One is the HARVEST MOUSE. It weaves a round nest and lives

Harvest Mouse

Deermouse

outdoors. Some kind of DEERMOUSE is found in almost every part of North America. These delicate and beautiful little animals are also called WHITE-FOOTED MICE. They are very nimble. When excited, most kinds drum on the ground with their front feet.

Some kinds of rats are quite small and look like large mice. Others are big. The head and body may be a foot long and the scaly tail even longer than that.

HOUSE RATS—like house mice—live closely with people. Where people go, the rat follows. It crosses the ocean on ships. It travels across the land on trains.

There are two common house rats in North America. Both are natives of the Old World. The BLACK RAT first arrived with the explorers. The BROWN RAT arrived around 1775. Both went westward with the pioneers.

The brown rat is also known as the NORWAY RAT and the HOUSE RAT. It is a big rat with coarse fur and large, naked ears. There is a little hair on its tail, and the tail is shorter than the body. Brown rats breed almost as fast as house mice. This rat is active all year and swims well. It eats garbage, grains, vegetables, meat, packaged foods, soap, eggs, and young birds. It gnaws the covering from electric

Norway Rat

Black Rat

wiring, sometimes causing fires. It needs a lot of drinking water. And it will gnaw through a lead pipe to get water.

The black rat is more slender, and its tail is longer than its body. It is a better climber than the brown rat, and it is very much at home on ships. Together these two rats cause millions of dollars' worth of damage in the world each year. Their fleas have spread diseases over whole continents.

Tamed strains of the brown rat are much used in laboratory studies of medicine. They are also kept as pets. These animals are often white in color.

One of the most interesting New World rats is the WOOD RAT. It is also called the PACK RAT, the TRADE RAT, and the CAVE RAT. It has large hairy ears, soft fur, and a long hairy tail. It eats mostly plant matter. In the West, wood rats build houses that look like small beaver lodges. A house may be on the ground, in a tree, or in a rocky place. Wood rats are collectors. They are very fond of shiny things—coins, watches, spoons, buttons, bits of tinfoil or glass. They pick up shiny things and take them home. (You can find many interesting things in a wood

rat's house.) On the way home, a wood rat may see something else it likes. It lays down what it is carrying and picks up the new thing. That is why it is sometimes called a trade rat.

Wood Rat

Mink

Mink

A mink is a member of the weasel family. It has a long, slender body and short legs. It has soft, thick underfur that is overlaid with long, glistening, dark hairs. Mink are highly valued for their fur. Some are trapped wild for their fur. Others are raised on mink ranches.

There are two main kinds of mink. One lives in the New World and one in the Old World. New World mink are found in Alaska, Canada, and all parts of the United States except the Southwest.

Like the weasel, a mink is a fearless fighter and an expert hunter. It hunts mice, rats, and rabbits. In summer it lives near water. It then hunts muskrats, marsh birds, and young snapping turtles. It eats frogs and shellfish and can catch fish.

Mink are active mostly at night. Sometimes a mink is cornered by an owl, fox, or wildcat. The mink screams, spits, and hisses. It gives off a powerful scent from glands near its tail.

Usually 5 to 8 mink are born in a litter. The young are very playful. They follow their parents until late summer. Then the family breaks up and the young go off on their own.

Moles

Day and night, moles are hard at work digging tunnels. A mole's front legs end in paddlelike hands with big claws. A mole shovels its way through the soil by using its front legs. It digs with a swimming motion something like the breast stroke. The paws dig through the soil and push it backward under the mole's body. When the soil piles up, the mole digs a shaft to the surface. Then it pushes the dirt out. The dirt forms a mound, or molehill.

Gardeners do not like molehills. But moles are often helpful to gardeners. They eat many harmful insects. The hardworking mole may eat its own weight in insects during one day's digging. The digging loosens the soil, which is often good for plants.

An animal that lives underground does not need to see very well. Most moles have small eyes and poor sight. Some kinds cannot see at all. But moles do have excellent senses of touch and smell.

Moles make two sets of tunnels. The tunnels we see are the upper ones. A mole makes these while looking for food. Its back pushes up the soil. The deeper tunnels are 1 to 2 feet below the surface. These connect with the food tunnels and serve as "streets" to the nests.

A mother mole usually has a litter of 2 to 5 young. The young are born in a nest of grass underground.

There are many kinds of mole in the world. The COMMON GARDEN MOLE is found in eastern North America. TOWNSEND'S MOLE lives near the Pacific coast. The strangest mole of all is the AMERICAN STAR-NOSED MOLE. Its nose is surrounded by 22 fleshy "fingers" that grow out like petals on a flower. The star-nosed mole is an expert swimmer and diver. It gathers some of its food in the water. The fleshy fingers are in motion as the mole seeks food.

Common Garden Mole

Townsend's Mole

Star-Nosed Mole

69

Mongooses

Mongoose

A mongoose is a small mammal that is expert at killing cobras. It will attack these poisonous snakes, which are several times its own length. The mongoose threatens the snake. The snake rears and strikes. The mongoose dodges. The snake strikes again. The mongoose plunges forward. It bites the snake at the back of the head. When the snake is dead, the mongoose eats it.

Mongooses are also good at killing rats. They are kept as rat-killers in some parts of the world. But they can also be a big problem. About 100 years ago mongooses were brought to islands in the West Indies to kill rats. The rats soon moved into the trees. And the mongooses took to eating eggs, chickens, and small animals that men needed. They became as big a pest as the rats. (The United States will not allow anyone to bring a mongoose into the country.)

Most kinds of mongoose live in Africa. Some live in Asia and southern Europe. They make their homes in burrows and are active by day.

Mongooses are members of a large family of meat-eating mammals. All these mammals are native to the Old World. Most are quite small. Many have claws like a cat's that can be drawn back into the paws. Most people have never heard of these mammals. But two you may read about are the CIVETS and GENETS.

Genet

African Civet

Monkeys

There are about 130 kinds of monkey in the world. Of these, 61 kinds are found in Asia and Africa. Together they are called Old World monkeys. The other 69 kinds are found in Central and South America. They are called New World monkeys.

The Old World monkeys all belong to one family. But the different kinds do not look much alike. Tails, snouts, and fur can be long or short. Some kinds have patches of skin that are bright red, blue, or purple. Some live in trees, while others spend most of their time on the ground.

The MACAQUES form a big group of Old World monkeys. Most kinds of macaque are about the size of a fox terrier. All have cheek pouches, where they store and carry food for short times. They live in troops. Strong and brave, they defend themselves well when attacked.

One of the best-known macaques is the RHESUS MONKEY of India. Active and playful, it is a favorite in ZOOS and circuses. This monkey is also used in medical research—in making polio vaccine, for example.

The BARBARY APE is another famous macaque, which is not an ape but a monkey. It is like an ape only because it has no tail. The Barbary ape lives in North Africa. It also lives on Gibraltar, where it was taken many, many years ago.

Barbary Ape

The CRAB-EATING MACAQUE lives in Malaysia and the Philippines. At low tide, it goes along the beach looking for crabs and other shellfish. It likes to eat them. This long-tailed monkey is a good swimmer and diver. If frightened, a whole tribe may dive into a river and swim across.

Rhesus Monkey

Guenon

Macaque

The PIG-TAILED MACAQUE of Sumatra is easily tamed when young. Natives teach it to climb coconut trees and drop nuts down to them.

Guenon

The GUENONS are another large group of African monkeys. Many kinds have beards. Some have brightly colored fur and skin. These slender monkeys travel through the trees in bands.

Langur

LANGURS are common monkeys in Asia. They are slender monkeys that live mostly in trees. But they can gallop on the ground at speeds up to 23 miles an hour. They eat fruits, flowers, and leaves. They are sometimes called LEAF MONKEYS.

In Borneo there is a very odd-looking monkey. It is called the PROBOSCIS, or LONG-NOSED, MONKEY. A male has a large nose that sticks out from his face. When excited, he makes his nose larger. This monkey's call sounds like the honk of a goose.

Proboscis Monkey

The largest monkeys are the baboons, which live in Africa.

See also: BABOONS

New World monkeys are smaller than their Old World relatives. They are very nimble in trees. And many have tails that can be used for grasping things. Like other monkeys, these eat mainly plant leaves, fruits, insects, and spiders. Most of them sleep during the night and are active by day.

The New World monkeys are grouped in two families.

MARMOSETS and TAMARINS make up one family. These monkeys are all quite small. They use their hands to catch or pick food. One kind has a mane on its head and shoulders. Some have tufts of hair on their ears.

There are many kinds of monkey in the other family. Here are just a few of them.

The DOURICOULI is the only New World monkey that is active at night. Like most night animals, it has very large eyes and sees well in the dark. It runs along tree limbs and leaps from branch to branch. It hunts through trees for fruits, leaves, insects, spiders, birds, and small mammals. It makes about 50 different sounds. Its danger call is "Wook!"

The largest New World monkeys are the HOWLERS. They are famous for their loud howls, which can sometimes be heard 2 miles away. Bands of up to 40 howlers travel among the treetops. A howler's thick, strong tail can be used for grasping limbs or food.

Douricouli

Howler

The UAKARIS are the only short-tailed American monkeys. Small bands of uakaris live among the tops of tall trees. They are much quieter than most monkeys. A uakari has a naked, red face. Its coat may be reddish brown, white, or brown and black.

The skinny SPIDER MONKEYS have very long legs, fingers, and tails. The tail can be used as a fifth hand. These monkeys travel in small groups. Scientists report that spider monkeys break off branches and try to drop them on people below.

Uakari

Spider Monkey

73

The CAPUCHIN MONKEY is active, intelligent, and full of mischief. It is often seen in zoos and circuses. In the wild, these monkeys travel in bands, chattering and shrieking. They are generally good-tempered. But like all monkeys, a capuchin may suddenly fly into a rage and bite a friend.

Lemur

Other Relatives

There are six families of other mammals that are related to the monkeys. All live only in the Old World. These mammals are less highly developed than the monkeys. Their brains are smaller. They do not have much curiosity. Most cannot use both eyes at the same time to look at one thing.

One family is made up of the TARSIERS. They live on islands of the East Indian region. A tarsier is so small you could hold one in your hand. Tarsiers have huge, owl-like eyes and froglike legs. They have long fingers and toes. At night a tarsier leaps about in bushes and trees, searching for food. Its main food is insects. It watches an insect, then leaps forward and seizes the insect with its hands.

Three families are made up of LEMURS. All live on the island of Madagascar, off eastern Africa. The smallest kind of lemur is the size of a mouse. The largest is the size of a medium-size dog. Most kinds of lemur live in trees.

Another family takes in the LORISES and POTTOS of Africa and Asia. These animals have short ears and short tails (or no tails). They climb trees slowly but surely.

TREE SHREWS make up the sixth family. They are the least highly developed of all. Some of these small animals look rather like squirrels. All have long noses. All have claws on their toes. They eat fruits and insects. When eating, they sit up and hold their food between their hands. "Tree shrews" is not a good name for these mammals. They are not shrews, and many do not live in trees.

A bull moose is the largest deer on earth. He is a giant who stands $7\frac{1}{2}$ feet high at the shoulder and sometimes weighs up to 1,800 pounds. His antlers alone may weigh 85 pounds. His stiltlike legs are $4\frac{1}{2}$ feet long. Often his long legs are a help in getting food. By standing on his hind legs, he can pull down branches growing 12 feet above the ground. Long legs are also good for wading. And a moose is fond of eating water lilies and other plants that grow in water.

Unlike other deer, the bull moose takes only one mate at a time. During the mating period he is ready to fight any other bull. When he hears one, he goes off at a trot. He swings his antlers, perhaps beating them against trees. A terrible battle may follow, as the two giants fight with their antlers.

Moose are found in Alaska, Canada, and some northern states. The North American moose has a close relative in northern Europe. Europeans call this deer an ELK.

Moose

Mountain Lions

Mountain lions are cats with many names. You may hear them called COUGARS, PANTHERS, and PUMAS. Some of their other names are CATAMOUNTS, PAINTERS, AMERICAN LIONS, and INDIAN DEVILS.

Mountain lions are fairly large cats. Most are 6 to 7 feet long. But from his nose to the tip of his tail, a large male may measure almost 10 feet. He may weigh more than 200 pounds. The mountain lion is a New World cat. Among American cats, only the jaguar is bigger. Mountain lions are now found mostly in western North America and in Central and South America.

The mountain lion usually hunts by night. Moving silently through the dark, it tracks its prey. Nearing, it suddenly bounds forward and kills. Mountain lions usually hunt deer and small mammals. They sometimes prey on horses, cattle, pigs and sheep. That is why they have been much hunted.

In spring a female chooses a cave or ledge for her den. Here her 2 to 4 cubs are born. The mother nurses and washes her cubs. She leaves them only to search for food. Young cubs have light brown fur with dark spots. As they grow older, they shed their spotted fur.

For the first few months the cubs play like kittens. They chase each other. They pounce on pebbles. By the age of 3 months they are eating meat that their mother brings home. Then they start to go hunting with her. They stay with their mother until they are a year or two old.

Mountain Lion

Mouse
See Mice and Rats

Mules
See Donkeys

Musk-oxen

The musk-ox lives in northern Canada and Greenland. It lives through the Arctic winter without shelter. Its big body is covered with thick fur. The outer coat is a layer of long hairs that reach to its ankles. These hairs shed rain and snow. The undercoat is made of fine, soft fur. It is so thick that it keeps the animal warm.

A musk-ox looks clumsy. But it moves easily and quickly on its broad hooves. The hooves spread. Their sharp edges cut into or grip the ground. Musk-oxen can run over crusted snow or rocky ground.

In the short Arctic summer musk-oxen feed on grasses and other plants. When autumn comes, the musk-oxen move into the hills. In some places the wind blows away the snow. Here the musk-oxen feed on dried, frozen plants. They can also paw away snow to find food.

A baby musk-ox is born in April or May. The Arctic is still full of snow and ice and biting winds. The calf huddles beneath its mother for warmth. In summer it learns to eat plants.

Sometimes wolves or bears try to attack musk-oxen. The herd backs into a circle, with their heads facing out. From time to time a bull dashes out to attack the enemy. A man with a rifle is the only enemy musk-oxen cannot defeat.

Musk Ox

Muskrats

A muskrat is a large, sturdy rodent (gnawing mammal). It is found in most parts of North America. It is a native of the New World, but it has been taken to the Old World. Muskrats are valued for their thick, shiny fur.

Muskrats make their homes in marshes, lakes, ponds, rivers, and streams. They swim by paddling with their webbed hind feet. They are very good swimmers. When there is danger, they dive. They can stay underwater for about 12 minutes.

Some muskrats build houses out of reeds. The houses look something like piles of weeds. A house is usually built on an island that the muskrat has made. Underwater tunnels lead to the house.

Other muskrats dig dens in the bank of a stream or pond. A muskrat starts by digging an underwater tunnel. The tunnel leads up into the bank. There the muskrat

Muskrat and young

makes its den. Later it may build more tunnels to the den. Muskrats are preyed on by many meat-eating mammals. Tunnels are the road to safety.

Muskrats eat mostly plants. They also eat clams, fish, and small water creatures. Each muskrat usually lives by itself. A female has several litters of 5 to 7 young each year.

Okapi
See Giraffes

Opossums

The opossum is the only mammal in North America that carries its babies in a pouch. At birth opossum babies are tiny. They are so tiny that 24 would fit in a teaspoon. They climb through their mother's fur into her pouch. Each attaches itself to a nipple. The nipple swells in its mouth. Mother and babies are now firmly attached. The babies stay there feeding.

By the time they are 10 weeks old, the babies are about the size of mice. They can leave the pouch and crawl about. They ride on their mother's back when she goes hunting. As they get bigger, she staggers under their weight. A mother opossum is not a very large animal.

The COMMON, or VIRGINIA, OPOSSUM is about the size of a house cat. Its paws look like tiny hands. They can be used for grasping things. An opossum can hang from a branch by its front feet or its hind feet. The scaly tail is sometimes used as a fifth hand. The tip can be used for grasping things.

Opossums usually live where there are trees. They are good climbers. They may sleep by day in the branches of trees. They also hunt for some of their food in trees. Opossums eat insects, mice, toads, birds, berries, and fruits.

An opossum builds its nest on the ground, often in a hollow stump. To make the nest, the opossum gathers dry leaves.

It picks up the leaves in its mouth. Using its feet, it packs the leaves into a bundle. Then it curls the tip of its tail around the bundle. It carries the bundle in its tail to the nest.

Opossums are famous for playing dead. Faced with danger, an opossum falls over. Its eyes are shut. Its tongue hangs out. It looks dead. The enemy is puzzled by this. Usually it goes away and leaves the opossum alone. Then the opossum recovers and wanders off. People used to think opossums played dead on purpose. Now scientists say this is not so. Threatened, an opossum goes into a state of shock, or faints. It cannot help falling over and looking dead.

The Virginia opossum is found in many parts of the United States and southern Canada. Central and South America have several kinds of opossum. None are found in the Old World.

Opossum

Orangutans
See Apes

Otters

Young or old, river otters like to play. Their favorite kind of play is sliding. In summer they slide down the bank of a stream into the water. In winter they slide on snow. Sometimes a whole family takes turns at sliding.

An otter can move well on land. But it is most at home in the water. Its sturdy body is streamlined for slipping through water. Its broad tail serves as a rudder. Its webbed feet are paddles. A coat of thick fur keeps the otter warm. An otter can cruise at 6 miles an hour. It can go much faster if it must.

Otters are good at fishing. They catch and eat fish, shellfish, frogs, turtles, and similar creatures. They also eat snakes, rabbits, water birds, muskrats, worms, and insects.

Some river otters live on shore. They make dens in hollow logs or under bushes. Most river otters make their den at the edge of the water. The den may have two entrances, one under water and one above. The den is lined with moss and dry leaves. Here 2 or 3 young are born each year. When they are about 3 months old, the mother teaches them to swim. The father helps and also plays with the pups.

There are about 12 kinds of river otter in the world. One kind lives in many parts of North America. Otters are members of the weasel family and are valued for their fur.

River Otters

Sea Otter

The biggest otter is the SEA OTTER. It is found only along the shores of the North Pacific. A full-grown male may be 6 feet long and weigh 75 pounds.

The sea otter spends most of its life afloat. It likes to live near rocky shores where there are beds of the seaweed called kelp.

When it is in a hurry, the sea otter swims on its belly. Mostly it floats on its back. From time to time it stands upright in the water. Shading its eyes with its paws, it looks about. At night it sleeps in the kelp, which keeps the otter from drifting. The sleeping otter may cover its eyes with its paws.

A sea otter eats fish, crabs, mussels, sea urchins, clams, and other kinds of sea life. It dives to find food. While eating, it floats on its back and uses its chest as a table. A young sea otter usually crushes the shells between its back teeth to get at the food inside. An older sea otter may bring up a stone from the bottom. It lays the stone on its chest. Then it opens the shells by pounding them on the stone.

Baby sea otters are born in the water. A mother takes very good care of her baby. She carries it and nurses it on her chest. She plays with it. She tosses it in the air and catches it. She licks it and washes it. When she must dive for food, she leaves the baby hidden in a bed of kelp. Alarmed, she takes the baby under one arm and dives.

Pandas

Giant Panda

The GIANT PANDA is found in the high mountains of southwestern China and eastern Tibet. It is bear-shaped and bear-sized. But its closest relatives are the raccoons.

The giant panda lives in thick forests of bamboo. In winter the black-and-white animal can hardly be seen among the black shadows on the white snow. The panda lives mostly on the ground. It climbs a tree only if chased by an enemy.

Bamboo shoots and roots are the giant panda's main food. (It also eats other plants, fish, and small mammals.) Most of its waking time is spent eating. A giant panda is awake and active for 10 or 12 hours a day. The pads on its front feet can be used to grasp food. They work something like fingers.

The LESSER PANDA is a much smaller animal. It is about the size of a large house cat. It looks something like a raccoon. The lesser panda lives in the forest-covered mountains of northern India and western China. It usually sleeps during the day. Sometimes it sleeps curled up. Then it puts its tail over its head, like a dog or cat. Sometimes it sleeps sitting up. Then it tucks its head between its front paws, like the American raccoon. The lesser panda eats mostly bamboo sprouts, grass, roots, fruits, and acorns. It may also eat eggs, birds, and mice. One or two young are born in spring. The lesser panda is a gentle, friendly animal that tames easily.

Lesser Panda

Pangolins

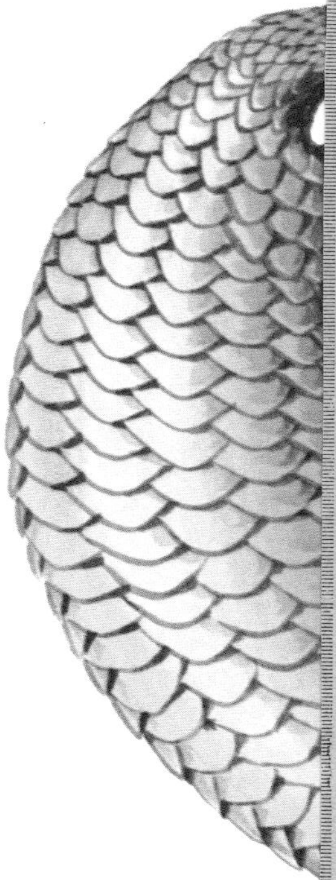

Pangolin

termites. A pan-
loes have a long,
rs food on its
ite nests with its

ds of pangolin.
ts of Africa and
live in burrows
mother pangolin
ack or tail.
es called SCALY

Panthers

ther" as another
ome use it only
call these ani-

"panther" as a
ion.
NTAIN LIONS

Peccaries

See *Pigs*

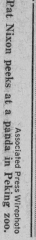

Pat Goes Sightseeing & Taste-Testing

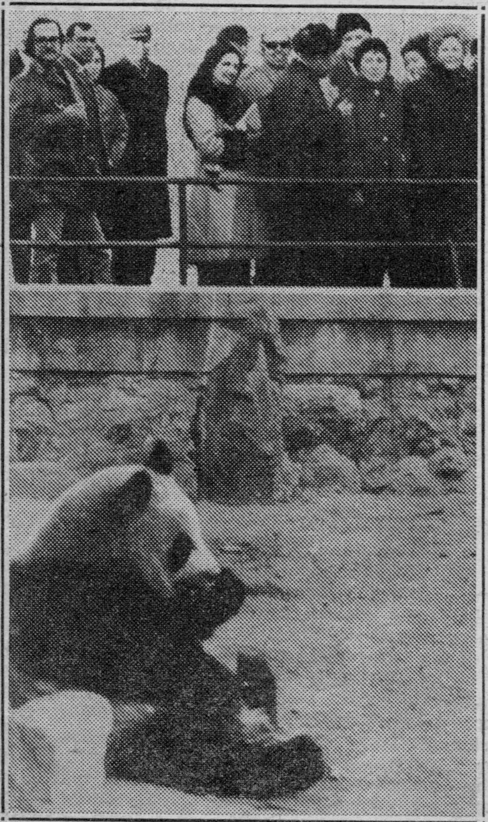

Associated Press Wirephoto

Pat Nixon peeks at a panda in Peking zoo.

By HUGH MULLIGAN

Peking, Wednesday, Feb. 23 (AP)—Pat Nixon got an inside look at how the Chinese masses live and work today when she paid a visit to the giant Evergreen People's Commune in Peking's northwestern suburbs, where 40,000 persons live in 9,000 households.

Then in the afternoon there was a tour of a Peking glass factory employing 530 workers.

Her schedule arranged for her to rejoin President Nixon for an evening gymnastic presentation at Peking Capital Stadium.

Yesterday, the first lady made a tasting tour of the kitchens of the famed Peking Hotel, visited the elaborate Summer Palace on a frozen lake outside the capital and watched a revolutionary ballet in the Great Hall of the People.

She also paid a surprise call to the Peking zoo and announced that Premier Chou En-lai is giving a pair of pandas to the United States in appreciation for two Canadian musk oxen the Nixons are sending their hosts. The gifts will provide the United States with its first pandas in decades.

'The President Loves Chinese Food'

In the evening the first lady joined her husband and went to a revolutionary ballet with the wife of Mao Tse-tung.

At the Peking Hotel earlier, Mrs. Nixon maintained a tradition of kitchen diplomacy when she nibbled at Chinese delicacies in a spotless kitchen.

The hotel's 115 chefs whipped up goldfish in white sauce, egg rolls on seaweed, steamed baby birds in clam shell pastry and other gourmet treats for the noonday session.

"The President loves Chinese food," Mrs. Nixon told the wives of top Chinese officials who accompanied her on the kitchen tour. "I'd love to try some of these dishes on my friends but I'm afraid I don't have the right equipment."

She finally turned chopsticks down on further sampling, and said, "All I seem to be doing all day is eating. I don't want to buy all new clothes when I get back."

The President and first lady were feted Monday night at a sumptuous eight-course banquet followed by rounds of toasts.

Mrs. Nixon's visit to the commune afforded her the opportunity of seeing one of the pillars of China's program to further the revolution. A commune is an organization of as many as 100 villages with a population sometimes numbering 50,000 or more. It is a political unit in itself, with its own government, military and judicial systems.

The concept is peculiar to the Chinese Communist system. It started with land reforms immediately after Mao Tse-tung took power, when landlord properties were seized and redistributed.

Pigs

Domestic Pigs

Young farm pigs are fun to watch. They are friendly, lively, and intelligent. They are very good at discovering how to get out of a pen. Once out, they have a fine romp. And they can run very fast—as you may know if you've chased one. Like all pigs, they love to eat. They plunge their heads and front feet into their food and gobble it down. But they keep themselves clean. Pigs are not dirty animals.

A male pig is called a boar. A female is a sow. "Hogs" is just another name for pigs. Farm pigs are raised for meat. They are easy to fatten up. And a sow has 2 or 3 large litters a year.

FARM PIGS look much like wild pigs. A pig is a hoofed mammal with a barrel-shaped body. Most kinds have a thin covering of bristly hairs. They have a long, pointed head that ends in a flattened snout. The snout is very useful. A pig uses it for pushing things aside and for digging food out of the ground.

Most farm pigs are probably descended

from the wild boar of Europe, Asia, and North Africa. The WILD BOAR stands about 3 feet high at the shoulder and may weigh 350 pounds or more. It has four tusks. Two grow from each jaw. Wild boars eat mostly plant food—roots, nuts, grain, and plant stems. They use their tusks and snouts to dig some of their food out of the ground. Wild boars travel in bands. They are quick-moving and good swimmers. They like to wallow in mud for hours at a time. A female has one or two litters a year. The young are striped, although the parents are not. Later the young shed their striped coats.

Many other kinds of wild pig live in Asia and Africa. One of the strangest looking is the WARTHOG of Africa. It has a big snout and long, curved tusks. Its body is covered with a thick mane of coarse hair. The male has lumps, or "warts," on his face.

There are no true wild pigs in the New World. Certain pigs, called RAZORBACK HOGS, live wild in the southeastern United States. But they are really farm pigs that escaped.

Wild Boar

The New World does have a family of wild, piglike animals called PECCARIES. They are related to pigs. But they are smaller and have a thick coat of bristly hair. When they are frightened, they give off an unpleasant scent. Two kinds of peccary live in Central and South America. One of them is sometimes seen in the United States near the Mexican border. It is called the COLLARED PECCARY.

Warthog

Peccary

85

Pikas

A pika is a small animal that looks something like a guinea pig. Most pikas live in rocky areas. They make nests among rocks.

A pika spends its time gathering grass, weeds, and other plants. It may even climb a tree and cut twigs from a low branch. This plant material is its food. The pika carries bundles of food back to its nest area. There it makes a kind of haystack, which dries in the sun. The dried plants become the pika's winter food.

Pikas have a whistling call. They give this call during the day and sometimes at night. A pika colony is a rather noisy place.

Pikas have a number of names. They are also called CONIES, ROCK RABBITS, WHISTLING HARES, and HAYMAKERS.

There are several kinds of pika. Most live in mountains of western North America, eastern Europe, and Asia. They are closely related to rabbits and hares.

Pika

Platypuses

The platypus has a furry coat, webbed feet, and a bill that looks like a duck's. The female lays eggs and feeds her young on milk. All told, the platypus is one of the strangest mammals in the world.

A platypus' home is a burrow dug in the bank of a stream. At dawn and at twilight the platypus waddles out to feed. At the water's edge, it closes its beady eyes and dives to the bottom of the stream. Its leathery bill is full of nerve endings. The platypus uses its bill to find small creatures that live in water. Then it comes to the surface and eats what it has found.

A mother digs a special burrow for laying eggs. In it she builds a nest of leaves and grass. She lays two eggs. They have soft shells and are dull white in color. For about two weeks the mother stays curled around her eggs, keeping them warm. She makes only brief trips out of the burrow. Then the babies break out of the eggs. The mother goes off to feed and to clean herself.

At first the babies get no food. Then milk starts to ooze from pores on the mother's stomach. The young lick it off the mother's fur and skin.

The platypus lives only in Tasmania and eastern Australia. It is sometimes called a DUCKBILL.

Platypus

Pocket Gophers

A pocket gopher spends much of its life digging tunnels. It digs with its front teeth and its claws. It uses its four huge front teeth to loosen soil. Its lips close behind the teeth. This way the gopher can gnaw dirt without getting any in its mouth. Once the soil is loose, the gopher digs with its big front claws.

When a gopher is digging, it makes a shaft to the surface. Then it pushes the loose earth to the surface of the ground. When it is not using the shaft, it plugs the opening with dirt. In loose, sandy soil a gopher may tunnel 200 to 300 feet in a single night.

Pocket gophers dig two sets of tunnels: deep ones and shallow ones. The gopher gets its food in the shallow tunnels. It

Pocket Gophers

Prairie Dogs

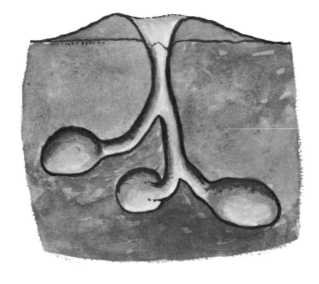

Prairie Dog

A prairie dog is not a dog. It is a rodent, or gnawing mammal. It is a sort of burrowing squirrel, and it is famous for its burrows. There used to be many more prairie dogs. Their burrows formed underground towns, with miles and miles of tunnels and dens. Several thousand prairie dogs lived in each of these towns. Today there are fewer prairie dogs, and the towns are smaller.

A prairie dog spends much of its time taking care of its burrow. The entrance goes almost straight down for 3 to 16 feet. Then it levels off into a tunnel. Rooms open off the tunnel. In one of these a mother makes a grass-lined nest. Here her young are born in late spring. Usually there are 5 young in a litter.

Earth from the tunnels and rooms is piled up around the entrance. It keeps water from running into the tunnels.

Prairie dogs come out by day. They feed on herbs and grass. They have many enemies. Badgers, coyotes, foxes, ferrets, and cats all eat prairie dogs. So do eagles and hawks. So the prairie dogs are always alert. They sit upright and look around. At any sign of danger, they scurry for home. They have several alarm calls. The kind of call tells whether the enemy is coming from the land or the air. There is also an all-clear call. If there is no danger, prairie dogs make a yipping sound, like a bark.

Prairie dogs live only in North America. They are found on western plains and prairies.

Pronghorns

The pronghorn is one of the swiftest mammals alive. Covering the ground in great leaps, it can easily travel at 40 miles an hour. It can keep up this pace for about 5 miles.

The pronghorn is sometimes called an antelope. But it is not a true antelope. It is more closely related to sheep. The pronghorn is found only in western North America.

A pronghorn has large, keen eyes. It can see objects several miles away. At any sign of danger, the pronghorn throws up its head and stares. White hairs rise on its rump. They flash in the sun. This is a warning signal. It can be seen by other pronghorns a couple of miles away. In turn, they flash warning signals. All the pronghorns gather in a galloping band.

Running is one way a pronghorn defends itself. It can also fight with its sharp hooves. If chased by a coyote, it will stop and jab at its enemy. The coyote quickly draws back. The pronghorn runs on.

Its horns are hollow and pointed. They grow over cores of bone that are attached to the skull. The pronghorn is the only horned mammal that sheds its horns. (Deer shed their antlers. But antlers are not the same as horns.)

Young pronghorns are born in the spring. A mother usually has a litter of two fawns. By the time they are 4 days old they can run faster than a man. Soon they are nibbling at plants, as their parents do. They grow up in a herd of fawns and mothers.

Pronghorn

See Mountain Lions **Pumas**

Rabbits and Hares

Most people find it very hard to tell rabbits from hares. And no wonder! Both have long ears and short tails. Their front legs are short. Their hind legs are long. They move in hops and leaps. What's more, one kind of animal may be called by the other's name. A jack rabbit, for example, is not a rabbit. It is a hare.

In general, hares are bigger and have longer ears. Their legs are longer and they can jump higher. The young of hares and rabbits are different, too. Baby hares are born with their eyes open. They are covered with fur. And they are able to hop around. Baby rabbits are born with their eyes closed. They have no fur. And they cannot hop. They are helpless babies.

There is still one other difference between hares and rabbits. Hares make their nests in hollows. Most rabbits dig underground burrows. (The cottontail is one of the rabbits that docs not.)

There are rabbits and hares in almost every part of the world. In North America the best-known rabbit is the COTTONTAIL. There are many kinds of cottontail. But all are small animals with a fluffy, white tail. Before her babies are born, a mother cottontail finds a hollow or digs one. She lines it with grass and with fur that she pulls from her belly. Usually 4 or 5 babies are born at a time. The mother covers her helpless babies with grass and fur when she goes away to eat. By the time the babies are 2 weeks old, their eyes are open. They are covered with fur. And they are ready to leave the nest. Soon the mother cottontail will have more babies. She has several litters a year.

Cottontail

In Europe the best-known rabbit is the EUROPEAN RABBIT. It looks like a big cottontail. European rabbits dig burrows. Trails lead from the burrows to the feeding grounds, where the rabbits eat grass, leaves, twigs, and buds. Sometimes many rabbits live in the same area, and their trails and burrows are linked. Together all these trails and burrows are called a rabbit warren. Do you remember Peter Rabbit? He was a European rabbit. So are most of the rabbits that people raise in the United States.

European Rabbit

JACK RABBITS are hares that live in western North America. There are several kinds. All have very long ears and very long legs. The largest kind is the WHITE-TAILED JACK RABBIT, which weighs between 5 and 8 pounds. It moves along with several short hops and then a long leap. When chased, it can reach a top speed of 40 miles an hour. Every now and then, it leaps up in the air to see where its enemy is.

Jack Rabbit

93

Some years ago European hares were taken to Ontario. Since then they have spread south into the United States. These large hares are sometimes called jack rabbits.

The VARYING HARE lives in Alaska, Canada, and the northern United States. As winter nears, its fur turns white. The hare can hardly be seen in the snow. This hare has broad hind feet. They act as snowshoes, keeping the animal on top of the snow. The varying hare is also called the SNOWSHOE HARE and the SNOWSHOE RABBIT.

The varying hare is big. The ARCTIC HARE is even bigger. In winter its fur is snow-white except for the tips of its ears. They are black. The Arctic hare lives in northern Alaska, Canada, and Greenland. In the very far north, it may be white all year round.

European Hare

Arctic Hare

Varying Hare

Raccoon

It is easy to tell a raccoon when you meet one. This small animal has a black mask across its face, and black and gray rings on its tail. Its paws look like tiny hands. A raccoon can use its paws almost as well as a monkey can. Let loose in a house, a raccoon will search it thoroughly. A raccoon can open bureau drawers, unhook latches, and unscrew jars. Raccoons are intelligent animals and full of curiosity.

A raccoon is a good swimmer and likes to live near water. It uses its fingers to catch fish, frogs, and shellfish. Raccoons also like to eat eggs, birds, insects, mice, nuts, seeds, fruits, and corn on the cob. They are expert at getting the lids off garbage cans and looking for food.

Sometimes raccoons are seen "washing" their food. No one is sure why they do this. They seem to enjoy feeling the food underwater.

The seven kinds of raccoon live only in the Americas. Six live south of the United States. One kind is found from southern Canada through most of the United States. Raccoons are active mostly at night.

A mother raccoon usually has a litter of 4 babies. They are born in a den. The den may be in a hollow tree or under some tree roots. By the time they are 10 to 12 weeks old, the young are leaving the den. They follow their mother and learn how to gather food.

Rats

See Mice and Rats

Reindeer

Reindeer

Reindeer are big, tamed deer of the far north. For thousands of years the people of Lapland have been raising herds of reindeer. And a whole way of life has been built around these herds.

The Lapp, his family, and his herd spend winter in southern Lapland. Here the reindeer feed on twigs. They paw through the snow to get at the mosses and lichens that grow below. Then the winter snows begin to melt. The Lapps move north with the herd to mountain pastures. In autumn they take the herd south. Reindeer pull the family's sleds on these trips. Reindeer carry the packs. Reindeer meat is eaten fresh, frozen, and dried. Reindeer milk is churned into butter and made into cheese. Frozen reindeer blood is carried as food for the dogs. Reindeer hides become warm parkas, trousers, mittens, and moccasins. Reindeer antlers become knife handles and other objects. The family money comes from the sale of reindeer.

Reindeer were first tamed from herds of wild deer that early hunters found in the north. These deer were CARIBOU, and reindeer are simply a tame form of caribou. Herds of them still live in the north today. They are found in the New World and the Old World.

A caribou is a large deer with a mane. Its broad, flat hooves are good for walking on snow and on spongy ground. Both males and females have antlers. (This is true also of reindeer.) Caribou move about in herds. They feed on plants. Their summers are spent in the north, where they eat grasses, willow and birch leaves, berries, and lichens.

Rhinoceroses

African Black Rhinoceros

There are five kinds of rhinoceros. Two live in Africa, one in India, and two on islands of Southeast Asia. All are becoming very rare.

A rhinoceros is a very large mammal. The smallest kind weighs nearly a ton. The largest kind weighs almost 2 tons. A rhino has a huge body on short legs. Its skin is thick and tough and bristly. Some kinds have two horns growing on top of the nose. Other kinds have one horn. The horns are made of hairs that have grown into solid masses.

The best-known rhino is the AFRICAN BLACK RHINOCEROS, which is really brown in color. It lives in East Africa. A full-grown male stands 5 feet high at the shoulder and may weigh 3,000 pounds. If disturbed, the rhino is a fierce fighter. It can charge forward at speeds of up to 30 miles an hour. Almost no other animal will attack a rhinoceros. Man is its chief enemy.

Like all rhinos, the African black is a plant-eater. It feeds on leaves, twigs,

African White Rhinoceros

grasses, and other kinds of plants. Its upper lip plucks the food and draws it into the mouth. The rhino lives in a home area where there is food and water. It needs water for drinking. And it loves to wallow in mud—rolling and wading and splashing. It also loves to roll in dust. The black rhino is most active in early morning and early evening. It sleeps during the hot part of the day.

A baby black rhino is born about 18 months after its parents have mated. At birth it may weigh 75 pounds. It stays with its mother for at least 2 years.

Most animals keep away from a rhino. But certain birds alight on a rhino to eat the ticks and insects that get onto it. They also act as lookouts. They chatter and scold when they hear something coming. A rhino itself has good hearing and a keen sense of smell. But it does not see very well.

Indian Rhinoceros

Rodents

When people talk about rodents, they usually mean mice and rats. It is true that mice and rats are rodents. But that is only the beginning of the story. Squirrels, chipmunks, beavers, porcupines, woodchucks, guinea pigs, and hamsters are also rodents. So are many, many other mammals that most people have never heard of. There are thousands of kinds of rodents. Rodents outnumber all the other kinds of mammals in the world.

A rodent is a mammal that gnaws. The many kinds of rodents all have four chisel-shaped front teeth. These are the

Pocket Mouse

gnawing teeth. The upper and lower teeth grind against each other. They keep wearing down into a sharp cutting edge. But the teeth do not wear down to stubs. These four teeth grow throughout a rodent's life.

Rodents are alike in other ways. Most are small animals—the size of a rat or mouse. All eat plant food—roots, bulbs, leaves, fruits, seeds, and nuts. Some also eat eggs and insects and other small animals. Most rodents are short-lived. But in their short lives they have many young.

The pictures show you a few of the rodents you may not have seen.

See also: BEAVERS; CHIPMUNKS; GUINEA PIGS; HAMSTERS; LEMMINGS; MICE and RATS; MUSKRATS; POCKET GOPHERS; PORCUPINES; PRAIRIE DOGS; SQUIRRELS; WOODCHUCKS

Mountain Beaver

Kangaroo Rat

Cavy

Chinchilla

Capybara

Sables

See Martens

99

Sea Cows

In days gone by, sailors used to tell tales of mermaids they had seen. The head and shoulders of the mermaid rose out of the water. Sometimes one was seen cuddling a baby.

These figures were not mermaids but sea cows. And close up they were not very beautiful. A sea cow is a large animal with wrinkled gray skin. The face is covered with bristles. The mouth is wide and drooping. Its front legs are paddle-like flippers. There are no hind legs.

Sea cows are mammals that live in the sea. They are born in the sea. They spend their lives there or in rivers that empty into the sea.

Today there are two main types of sea cow. One is called the MANATEE and the other is called the DUGONG. Both are found only in warm, shallow waters. Both have been much hunted for their flesh and oil. And both are fairly rare.

Some manatees live off western Africa. Others live along the eastern coasts of the Americas. The American manatee is a quiet, slow-moving animal. Full-grown, it measures 8 to 12 feet long and weighs about a ton. It eats huge amounts of grasses and other water plants. The manatee plucks the plants with its lips and grinds them up between its teeth.

The manatee swims by pumping its broad tail up and down. It steers with its flippers. It can swim underwater for long distances. Sometimes it rests on the sea-bottom. It comes up for air several times an hour.

A baby manatee is born underwater. The mother lifts it to the surface on her back. She holds it in her flippers while nursing it. Fishermen say that mother manatees baby-sit for each other. One mother holds both babies while the other mother feeds.

Dugongs look much like manatees. They live in coastal waters of the Indian Ocean and the eastern Pacific.

Manatee

Sea Lions and Fur Seals

Together, the sea lions and the fur seals form a family called the EARED SEALS. All have small, outside ears on their heads. (The true seals do not have outside ears.)

There are 12 kinds of eared seal. The SEA LIONS have thin coats of short, coarse hair. A FUR SEAL has a thick coat of soft underfur topped by coarser hairs. (Fur seals have been much hunted for their fur.)

Every eared seal has a streamlined body with four flippers. The front flippers are longer than the hind flippers. An eared seal swims with its front flippers and steers with its hind flippers. When it leaves the water, it turns its hind flippers forward. It can walk on its flippers, but walking is difficult.

Most eared seals live in herds. They spend much of their time in the water, where they feed mostly on fish. Most eared seals live in the Southern Hemisphere. Four kinds are found off the western coast of North America.

The CALIFORNIA SEA LION is the best-known. This is the trained seal that you see in a zoo or circus. It is able to balance a big rubber ball on its nose. It can play a tune on a row of trumpets. It can sway and dance to music. Sea lions are bright and playful. They love attention and rewards. And so they are easy to train.

The male sea lion is about 8 feet long and weighs 500 to 600 pounds. Like all eared seals, a mother sea lion goes ashore when it is time for her pup to be born. A new-born pup is able to swim but does not wish to do so. The pups first swim in shallow pools near the shore. Later they

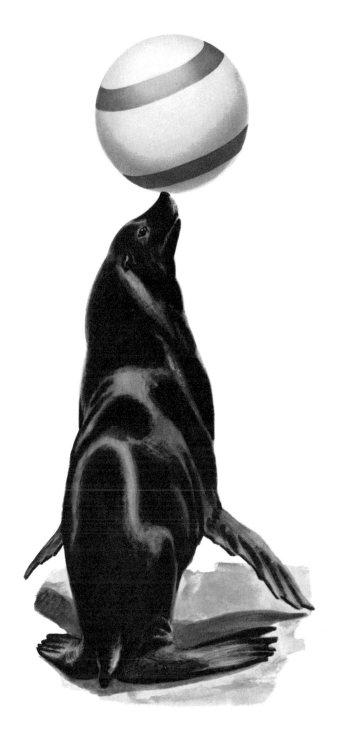

California Sea Lion

Steller's Sea Lion

go to sea with their mothers.

The ALASKAN, or NORTHERN, FUR SEAL spends much of the year at sea. The males roam the North Pacific, looking for food. The females travel much farther south, to waters far off the coasts of California and Mexico. In spring the fur seals head for the Pribilof Islands, near Alaska, or for islands near the coast of Asia. By early May the males are gathering on the beaches. Each stakes out a piece of beach as his own. In late June the females begin to arrive. They are almost ready to bear their young. Each male herds as many females as he can onto his beach. The females give birth to their young. Then they mate with the males.

Each pup is nursed by its mother. Several times a week the mother swims out to sea to feed. On her return she is able to find her own pup among the many on the beach. By the time they are 6 or 8 weeks old, the pups can swim. At 4 months they are finding their own food. Soon the females start south again, on the first half of their 6,000-mile round-trip. The pups go off to sea about the same time. But they do not travel with their mothers.

Alaskan Fur Seal

Seals have several names. Sometimes they are called TRUE SEALS. This is to set them off from the sea lions and fur seals. Sometimes they are called HAIR SEALS. This is because their bodies are covered with short, coarse hair. Sometimes they are called EARLESS SEALS. This is because they have no outer ear.

There are 18 kinds of seal, and they are found in many parts of the world. Seals are found in all the oceans. Some have even gone up rivers and taken to living in lakes.

In many ways, all these seals are alike. A seal has four flippers. The hind flippers are longer than the front ones. A seal swims with its hind flippers. It uses its front flippers for turning or balancing in the water. A seal often stands upright in the water. It does this by treading water with its front flippers.

The hind flippers reach out behind the seal. They cannot be turned forward. As a result, a seal cannot walk on its flippers. To move on land, a seal wriggles and hunches. Whenever possible, it rolls or slides. Even so, a seal can move surprisingly fast on land. For a short distance the crab-eater seal can wriggle faster than a man can run.

Most kinds of seal eat fish, shellfish, and small creatures that live in the water. The LEOPARD SEAL of the Antarctic eats other seals and birds. It often captures and eats penguins.

Seals usually live in groups. They leave the water to shelter on rocky or sandy coasts, on islands, or on big pieces of floating ice. Wherever they are, they are within quick reach of the water.

Seals must leave the water to breed and to bear their young. Most kinds of baby seal are born with a thick coat of woolly hair. Within a month, the baby sheds this coat. It grows an adult coat of coarse hair. A baby is born able to swim. But it does not go into the water at first. It stays ashore and nurses for several weeks. Then it starts to swim and to find its own food.

Guadalupe Fur Seal

Harbor Seal

The HARBOR SEAL is the most common kind in the Northern Hemisphere. It is a small seal with a somewhat doglike face. It does a lot of barking and grunting. When it wants to sleep, it crawls out of the water onto a ledge.

The two kinds of ELEPHANT SEAL are the largest. One lives around the Antarctic. The other lives off Mexico. The males may grow to be 20 feet long and weigh 8,000 pounds. A male has a snout, or trunk, about 15 inches long. When there is danger, he blows air into his trunk and trumpets loudly.

Ribbon Seal

Elephant Seal

Sheep

Domestic Sheep

For thousands of years people have been raising sheep for wool, hides, and meat. Today there are about 40 breeds of sheep. Most of them look like the sheep you know. They have long tails and coats of woolly fleece.

There are also several kinds of wild sheep. All live in the Northern Hemisphere. They do not look much like the sheep of farms and ranches. Wild sheep have short tails and coats of stiff hairs.

Two kinds of wild sheep live in North America. One is the ROCKY MOUNTAIN SHEEP, or BIGHORN. It lives in western mountains from Canada to Mexico. The other is the DALL SHEEP. It lives in Alaska and northwestern Canada. It is more slender than the bighorn. Both kinds of sheep have horns. The rams have huge, heavy horns that curl back and around.

These wild sheep live among ledges, cliffs, and steep slopes. They move about with sure-footed swiftness. They plunge down cliffs, leaping 20 feet at a time. They bounce from one ledge to another. Near the bottom they sail off into the air and land on all four feet. Their hooves are slightly hollow and have sharp edges. The hooves cling to rocks and keep the sheep from skidding.

Lambs are born in the spring. The mother sheep leaves the band with which she has been feeding. She climbs to a sheltered place. When the lamb is born, the mother stands guard over it for about a week. Then she takes it to the band. Soon all the lambs are nibbling leaves, grass, and flowers. They play together while the mothers feed and watch out for eagles and other enemies.

Rocky Mountain Goat

Dall Sheep

Shrews

Water Shrew

The PIGMY SHREW is the smallest mammal in North America. It is 3 inches long from the tip of its nose to the tip of its tail. And it weighs less than a dime. This tiny creature lives in Alaska, Canada, and some of the northern and eastern states. Still smaller shrews live in other parts of the world.

There are many, many kinds of shrew. None is very big. Most live on the ground. A few live in burrows and a few live in trees. Some kinds of shrew can swim. The AMERICAN WATER SHREW can skitter across the top of the water.

A shrew spends much of its time scurrying along the ground, hunting for food. It eats insects, such as moths and beetles. It also eats animals that are bigger than itself, such as mice. A tiny shrew eats huge amounts of food. It is a very active animal and its body burns up food quickly. It is also a very nervous animal. A loud noise, such as thunder, can frighten a shrew to death.

Shrews are the only mammals with a poisonous bite. Some of these animals have poison in their saliva. A shrew can kill a mouse by biting it. (The poison does no serious harm to man.)

A female shrew has 2 or 3 litters of young a year. As many as 10 young may be born in a litter. They are born in nests of grass hidden under leaves or logs.

Shrews send out a steady stream of high-pitched sounds. Possibly shrews find their food with these sounds, as bats and dolphins do. When the sounds hit something, they echo. The shrew may hear the echo and so learn where the food is.

Pigmy Shrew

Striped Skunk

Never frighten a skunk. If you meet one, stand still and be quiet. The skunk will probably go on its way. Skunks are easy-going animals. They defend themselves only when threatened. Even then, they give warning first. Faced with danger, a skunk growls and stamps its front feet. Then it raises its bushy tail. If the enemy still advances, the skunk acts quickly. It sprays the enemy with an evil-smelling liquid.

Muscles force the liquid out of two small openings at the base of the tail. A skunk uses only a little of the liquid at a time. It is armed for several shots. And it can hit an enemy that is 12 or 15 feet away. The spray has a terrible smell and taste. It stings the eyes. Usually one shot is enough to send an enemy howling away.

Water will take away the sting. But it won't take away the smell. If your dog is "skunked," scrub him with tomato juice. Then give him a bath. Skunked clothes can be washed in a pail of warm water mixed with a cup of ammonia. (But never use ammonia on a dog or other animal.)

Skunks live only in the Americas. The most common kind in North America is the STRIPED SKUNK. It lives in a hollow log or in a hole in the ground. Sometimes it lives under a building. It comes out at night to look for food. It eats insects, mice, snakes, and frogs. It also likes berries, fruits, grains, and eggs.

From 4 to 7 baby skunks are born at a time. When they are 6 weeks old, they begin to go out. They follow their mother as she looks for food. The family walks single file, with the mother leading her babies, one by one.

The SPOTTED SKUNK is smaller and lives in the United States, Mexico, and Central America. It is playful and full of energy. It can climb up fence posts, trees, and the walls of sheds. If it is threatened, it sometimes walks on its front feet, with its hind feet and tail in the air.

Spotted Skunk

Hooded Skunk

Hognosed Skunk

The HOODED SKUNK looks much like the striped skunk. It lives in the southwestern United States and in Central America. The HOG-NOSED SKUNK lives in the same areas and in South America. It is the largest skunk. It has a snout somewhat like a pig's. It uses its snout and claws to root and dig in the ground for food.

Skunks belong to the weasel family.

Sloths

Sloths live upside down in trees. A sloth has long, hooked claws at the ends of its toes. It hangs by its claws from a branch in a tree. If it must move, it travels slowly, hand over hand. Mostly, though, a sloth sleeps. It sleeps about 18 hours a day, hanging from a branch.

A baby sloth is born while its mother hangs upside down. At first it lives on her chest. Then it hangs from her neck. It finally begins to hang from a branch itself.

A sloth cannot stand up on its legs. On the ground it pulls itself along. But it swims well, with a kind of breast stroke. Sloths defend themselves by biting and clawing.

Sloths are brown or gray in color. But sometimes they appear bright green.

Two-Toed Sloth

This is because tiny green plants grow on the hairs of their fur. A green sloth is almost impossible to see in a tree.

There are two main types of tree sloth. One is called the TWO-TOED SLOTH. It is about as big as a medium-sized dog. It has two huge, curved claws on its hands. Its body is covered with shaggy hair. The sloth has very long arms and no tail. Sometimes its eyes are bright red. The sloth wanders slowly about in trees. It hooks leaves and fruits with a hand and then eats them.

The other type is the THREE-TOED SLOTH. It has three hooked claws on its front hands. It is slightly smaller and even less active. Both types live in the forests of Central and South America.

Three-Toed Sloth

Spiny Anteaters

Left alone, a spiny anteater shuffles along, looking for food. When it finds an ant or termite nest, it tears into the nest with its front claws. Its long, sticky tongue flicks in and out of its mouth. That is how it gathers insects.

If frightened, the spiny anteater buries itself with astounding speed. Digging with all four feet, it quickly sinks out of sight into the ground. An attacker sees only its back. And the back is covered with short, sharp quills.

Spiny Anteater

The spiny anteater is a mammal that lays eggs. A mother grows an extra piece of skin on her underside. It serves as a pouch. She lays one or two eggs. Then she carries the eggs about in her pouch. When they hatch, the mother carries her babies in her pouch. They feed by lapping up milk that oozes out of her skin.

The baby anteaters grow spines, or quills. When they are too spiny for comfort, the mother puts them out of the pouch. She hides them under bushes and comes to feed them. When her pouch is no longer needed, it disappears.

There are two main kinds of spiny anteater. They live in Australia, Tasmania, and New Guinea.

The only other egg-laying mammal is the platypus.

Squirrels

Gray Squirrel

The many, many kinds of squirrel can be sorted out into three main groups. These are the tree squirrels, the ground squirrels, and the so-called flying squirrels, which are really gliders.

TREE SQUIRRELS are the ones you see most often. They are small, long-bodied animals with bushy tails. Its tail is very important to a tree squirrel. The tail acts as a balancer when the squirrel is leaping from branch to branch. It is a warm blanket when the squirrel curls up on a cold night.

Tree squirrels are expert climbers. Most go up a tree trunk at a run. They scamper along branches and leap from tree to tree. A leaping squirrel spreads its legs, flattens its body, and stiffens its tail. It coasts through the air, lands, and is off about its business.

These squirrels make their homes in trees. They prefer a hollow trunk or limb as a home. Sometimes one builds a big nest of leaves and twigs. By day they are very busy looking for food. Tree squirrels eat mostly seeds, nuts, and fruits. Some kinds also eat insects and other small animals. Many kinds gather and store food for winter. Often they store food by burying it. No one is sure how squirrels find this food again. Perhaps they remember where they buried it. Perhaps they find it by smell.

Baby squirrels are born in spring or summer. They stay in the home for a while. Then they come out and play in the sunshine.

The GRAY SQUIRREL is a common North American tree squirrel. It is usually gray, but a few are black.

The RED SQUIRRELS are found in forests of Alaska, Canada, and the United States. They are very "talky" squirrels. They spend some time on the ground and may make burrows.

The FOX SQUIRREL is the largest American tree squirrel. It is found from the East Coast west to Texas and South Dakota. Most of the fox squirrels are reddish brown in color.

Fox Squirrel

GROUND SQUIRRELS are never found in the eastern half of North America. Some live as far east as Ohio, but most live in western North America. Some kinds look very like chipmunks, except that ground squirrels do not have stripes on their cheeks.

Red Squirrel

Columbian Ground Squirrel

111

Tigers

Siberian Tiger

Tigers live mostly in the forests of Asia. The largest ones live in the cold, snowy north. These are the SIBERIAN TIGERS. A big male may be more than 10 feet from his nose to the end of his tail. He may weigh 600 to 650 pounds. This tiger has long, thick fur that is pale in color. In warmer parts of Asia the tigers are smaller and more brightly colored. The tiger you usually see in a zoo or circus is an INDIAN TIGER. Sometimes it is called the BENGAL TIGER. It is a big handsome cat.

A tiger is hard to see in its forest home. Its stripes blend with the shadows and streaks of sunshine. A tiger likes to be near water. It needs water to drink. It also bathes in water and is a good swimmer. It hides by day and hunts by night.

A tiger usually hunts alone. It moves silently and quickly. It springs with ease and may cover 15 feet in one leap. Tigers hunt deer, wild pigs, and other hoofed mammals. Near villages tigers prey on cattle and goats. When a tiger has killed, it carries the victim to some hidden spot. There the tiger eats its fill. It may feed on the same animal for several days.

Usually 2 to 4 tiger cubs are born at a time. They are not ready to hunt for themselves until they are about a year old. By then they have learned to lie in wait and spring on a passing animal.

In zoos tigers sometimes breed with lions. If the father is a tiger, the young are called TIGONS. If the father is a lion, they are called LIGERS.

Indian Tiger

Vicuñas

See Llamas

Voles

See Mice and Rats

A walrus is a mammal of the sea. It has flippers instead of legs. The front flippers are long and oarlike. The walrus swims with them. Its top speed is about 15 miles an hour. Out of the water, a walrus can waddle along on all four flippers. It can also run. In this it is like its relatives the sea lions and fur seals.

A grown walrus is 8 to 12 feet long. It may weigh almost 3,000 pounds. It has only a few stiff hairs on its wrinkled hide. But it has a large mustache. The mustache is part of the walrus' sense of touch. It is useful for feeling things on the bottom of the ocean. That is where a walrus searches for food. A grown walrus also has two long tusks—teeth that grow down from the upper jaw. A walrus uses its tusks to defend itself. It uses them when it hauls itself out of the water onto ice. And it uses them when feeding. A walrus feeds by sinking to the bottom and digging in the mud and sand with its tusks. It digs for clams and other kinds of sea life. It cracks the shells between its back teeth.

Herds of walruses live in the Arctic Ocean. They are noisy animals that fill the air with bellowing and trumpeting. They spend part of their time in the water and part out. They haul themselves out onto rocky coasts, islands, and floating ice.

A baby walrus is born out of the water. It first goes to sea on its mother's neck. It clings with its flippers as she swims and dives. The young walrus nurses for about 2 years. By then it has grown teeth and tusks and can dig its own food.

Walruses are hunted by killer whales and polar bears. Their other enemy is man. Eskimos hunt walruses for their meat, fat, hides and tusks.

Walrus

Wapiti
See Deer

Warthogs
See Pigs

Weasels

All weasels are small, and all are fierce fighters. A weasel will attack animals its own size. It will attack smaller animals. And it will attack animals that are much bigger than it is. A weasel will even attack a man who happens to be standing between the weasel and its meal. Weasels are in turn eaten by larger mammals and birds.

A weasel has a long, slender body. It can slip into any burrow or hole that is big enough for its head. Some weasels can follow a mouse into its home. Weasels have entered chicken coops through knotholes. Some weasels are farm pests because of the chickens that they kill. But on the whole weasels are helpful to man. They keep down the numbers of mice, rats, and rabbits.

There are about a dozen kinds of weasel. Three are found in the New World. (The same three are also found in the Old World.) One of these is the SHORT-TAILED WEASEL, which is called a STOAT in the Old World. It is about the size of a chipmunk, but longer. The young are born in a ready-made den—a hollow under a log or stump, a rockpile, or a chipmunk den. Usually 4 to 7 young are born in a litter. This weasel is found in much of North America. In autumn many short-tailed weasels shed their brown coats. They grow white coats that hide them in the snow. When it turns white, the short-tailed weasel is called an ERMINE. Its fur is highly valued.

The LEAST WEASEL is about 10 inches long and may weigh as little as 1 ounce. It is found in Alaska, most of Canada, and some northern parts of the United States. This tiny weasel takes over a mouse nest and lines it with mouse fur. Like all weasels, it has scent glands at the base of its tail. It gives off an unpleasant odor when frightened.

The LONG-TAILED WEASEL is found from southern Canada into South America. It lives in fairly open areas and is active mostly at night. It is excellent at catching mice and rats.

Long-Tailed Weasel

Ermine

Least Weasel

Short-Tailed Stoat

116

Sulphur Bottom or Blue Whale

The BLUE WHALE is the largest animal in the world. It is between 70 and 100 feet long and weighs up to 125 tons. This giant mammal is found in the cold waters of the Arctic and the Antarctic. It feeds on tiny shrimplike creatures called krill. In a single meal a blue whale may eat some 5 million krill, weighing 2 tons.

There are about 90 kinds of whale. Scientists divide them into TOOTHED WHALES and BALEEN, or MUSTACHE, WHALES. The blue whale belongs to the baleen whales. These whales do not have teeth. Instead, they have long blades of horny material hanging from the upper jaw inside the mouth. The material is called baleen, or whalebone. A baleen whale takes in a mouthful of water and krill. Then it forces the water out through the baleen. The baleen acts as a strainer. The water goes out, but the food stays in the mouth.

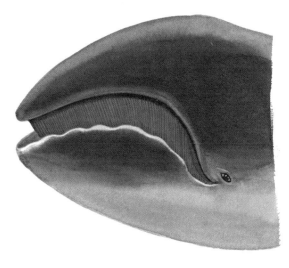

Baleen Whale

Toothed Whale

The largest numbers of krill are found in very cold waters. And that is where blue whales spend most of their time. But a mother swims thousands of miles to warmer waters before her baby is born. Like all whales, she swims by moving her broad tail up and down. At birth the baby is about 25 feet long. Under its skin is a thick layer of fat called blubber. This keeps whales warm. They are not covered with fur but have only a sprinkling of bristles.

Most baleen whales are very large. Scientists divide them in three groups: the FIN WHALES, the GRAY WHALE, and the RIGHT WHALES. The right whales were named in the early days of whaling. To whalers, they were the "right" whales to go after. They were slow swimmers. They did not fight when harpooned. They stayed afloat when killed. And they yielded large amounts of oil and whalebone. As a result, the right whales were almost wiped out.

Right Whale

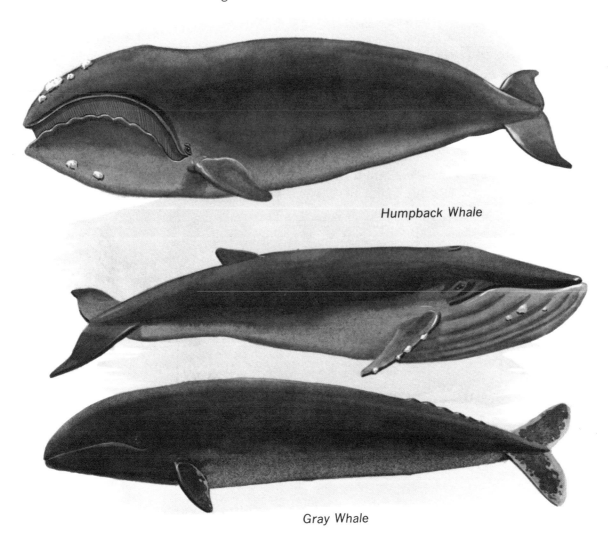

Humpback Whale

Gray Whale

All the baleen whales have two blow-holes on top of the head. The blowholes snap shut when the whale dives. They open when the whale surfaces to breathe. When a whale surfaces, it spouts. Many people think the whale is blowing water out of its lungs. But this is not so. The whale blows out a great lungful of warm, moist breath. When this breath meets the colder air, it condenses into water.

The toothed whales have only one blow-hole. And they are mostly smaller than the mustache whales. Only one toothed whale is really big. This is the giant SPERM WHALE, which is 44 to 60 feet long. It is the only source of ambergris. This waxy matter forms inside the whale, perhaps because of an upset stomach. It is used in making perfume.

Most of the toothed whales are DOL-PHINS and PORPOISES. All but a few are quite small—less than 15 feet long. One of the big dolphins is the PILOT WHALE. Another is the KILLER WHALE. Killer

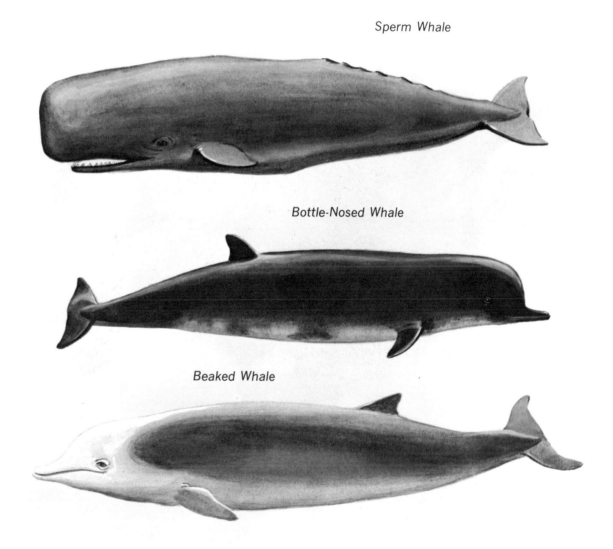

Sperm Whale

Bottle-Nosed Whale

Beaked Whale

119

whales are sometimes about 30 feet long. They are big, strong, and cunning. The other toothed whales eat fish and shellfish. The killer whale is the only one that eats warm-blooded prey. It eats small mustache whales, porpoises, seals, and penguins.

See also: DOLPHINS

Killer Whale

Wildcats

See Lynxes

Wolverines

Wolverine

A wolverine is a shaggy animal of the weasel family. It is found around the world in the far north.

The wolverine is not large—it weighs only 25 to 40 pounds. But it is fearless. It will attack almost any other animal. It drives bears and mountain lions from their kills, which it eats itself. It kills caribou and mountain sheep by leaping on them from a cliff or tree. It is strong enough to kill even elk and moose that are trapped in deep snow.

A wolverine usually lives by itself. It is active either day or night all year round. It sleeps and hunts, sleeps and hunts.

Each wolverine has its own area where it lives and hunts. Little is known about the family life.

Eskimos like to use wolverine fur on their parka hoods. Only a little moisture from the breath freezes on this fur. And it can easily be brushed off. This is not true of other kinds of fur.

Wolves

Wolves

Once there were wolves in most parts of the Northern Hemisphere. They were different sizes and colors. But most were the kind we call the GRAY, or TIMBER, WOLF. Men, however, have always feared wolves. So wherever men have gone, they have killed wolves. There are very few wolves left in Europe. Some packs still roam northern Asia.

The gray wolf has been killed off in North America except in the unsettled parts of Canada and Alaska. It is seen almost nowhere else. Another kind, the RED WOLF, may be seen in the southern United States. It lives in a few wild parts of Louisiana, eastern Texas, and Arkansas. The red wolf is smaller than the gray. Its coat is usually reddish, but it can be black. Black pups may be born in the same litter with red pups.

The gray wolf looks like a heavily built German shepherd dog. In color it is usually gray or tawny. But in the far north, its coat is pure white. Gray wolves are big, strong, and intelligent.

Wolves seem to mate for life. Wolf pups are born in early spring. They are born in a den that may be a cave or a burrow. Usually there are 4 to 6 pups in a litter. The mother and pups stay in the den. The pups nurse, and the father brings food to the mother. He stands guard outside the den.

When the pups are a month old, they start to leave the den and play outside. Soon they are eating solid food. Then both parents are kept busy finding food for their hungry, growing young. During the summer the pups learn to hunt by following their parents. By autumn they are able to hunt by themselves. But they usually stay with their parents for 2 or 3 years. During this time the parents have another litter or two of pups.

Red Wolves

Wolves hunt in packs. A pack is usually a family group. It is made up of a mother and father and the young from one or more litters. Sometimes relatives join the pack. Sometimes two different families join forces.

The pack follows wolf trails in its hunting. The trails reach over a wide area. A wolf pack on the hunt may travel several hundred miles. The wolves live wherever they happen to be. They have no fixed home. But they do go back to one area each year to bear their young.

Wolves are chiefly meat-eaters. Eyes, ears, and noses alert, they search for game. They eat what they find. In the far north they track caribou, attacking the young and the strays. Farther south they eat deer, moose, and other large hoofed mammals. If they find sheep and cattle, they will attack those. Wolves also hunt hares, rats, mice, squirrels, and other small mammals. They will eat insects and fruits.

Wolves may track their prey for hours. They move in a tireless trot, which they can keep up for miles. Finally, several wolves attack. Then the pack swarms over the prey and eats its fill. A wolf can eat 15 pounds of meat at a time. Leftover food is sometimes buried and eaten later.

Scientists think that our dogs are mostly descended from wolves. Wolves are also closely related to coyotes.

Woodchucks

In early morning the woodchuck leaves its burrow. It feeds on grass, clover, and other plants. Belly full, it stretches out in the shade and dozes. In late afternoon it feeds again. Then it goes back to its burrow. A woodchuck is a plump, somewhat lazy animal. It is a pest in the garden, but it makes a nice pet.

The burrow usually has several doors. One is a drop hole that goes straight down for a couple of feet. If startled, a woodchuck gives a shrill whistle. It may vanish down its drop hole. The woodchuck's burrow has several rooms. In one of them a mother woodchuck has 4 or 5 babies each spring.

In autumn a woodchuck grows very fat. When cold weather comes, it tucks itself away in its burrow. It sleeps through the winter. Its body draws on the fat for food.

The woodchuck is also called a GROUND-HOG. The story goes that it wakes up and comes out of its burrow on February 2. If the sun is shining, the animal sees its shadow. It goes back to sleep for six more weeks. And that means there will be six more weeks of winter. If the day is cloudy, the animal does not see its shadow. It does not go back to sleep. And that means an early spring. There is really no truth in this story. But February 2 is called Groundhog Day.

The woodchuck lives in most of Canada. In the United States it lives east of the Mississippi but not in the deep South. It has two close relatives in the West. They are called MARMOTS OR ROCK CHUCKS. Other kinds of marmot live in the Old World, north of the equator.

Woodchuck

Yaks

See Cattle

Zebras

A zebra is a type of wild horse that is found only in Africa. Zebras live in herds. The herds are usually small, with 10 or 12 members. As they move about grazing on grass, zebras often mix with other kinds of animals. They have even been seen feeding with ostriches. In the dry seasons zebras travel far, looking for grass and water. Then they may band together in big herds of up to a thousand.

Zebras are shy animals. When frightened, they run. They can run very fast—up to 40 miles an hour. But they will also fight to defend themselves. A zebra kicks backward with its hind feet and forward with its front feet. Its hooves can deliver powerful blows. Zebras also bite. Lions are about the only animals that attack zebras. Zebras are always on the lookout for this enemy. They have very good eyes and a keen sense of smell. A zebra's stripes can also be a help. In tall grass or in forests the stripes blend with the shadows. A zebra is very hard to see.

There are three main kinds of zebra. The biggest is called GREVY'S ZEBRA. It stands about $4\frac{1}{2}$ feet high at the shoulder and weighs between 500 and 600 pounds. The most common zebra is BURCHELL'S ZEBRA. It is found in many parts of Africa. The MOUNTAIN ZEBRA of South Africa is the rarest.

Many people have tried to tame zebras. Usually they have failed.

Burchell's Zebra

Grevy's Zebra

Mountain Zebra

The Orders of Living Mammals

There are many, many kinds of living things. To deal with them, scientists have sorted them into groups. The living things within each group are somehow alike.

One huge group is called the Animal Kingdom. Its members can be as different as a butterfly and an elephant. But they are all animals. In that way they are alike.

Within the Animal Kingdom the mammals form a large group. This group is called a class. Its members can be as different as an otter and an elephant. But all mother mammals have glands that produce milk. The young feed on the milk. In that way all mammals are alike. Then, too, almost all mammals have hair. That is another way they are alike. No other class of animal has hair or produces milk.

The class of mammals is made up of 18 smaller groups. These groups are called orders. The members of each order are somehow alike and somehow related. (Orders in turn are made up of smaller groups of more closely related mammals.)

The list that follows gives you the name of each order. It tells you how the members of an order are alike. And it arranges by order many of the mammals in this book.

Monotremata	This order is made up of egg-laying mammals. They are found only in Australia and neighboring islands. MEMBERS: *platypuses 86–87, spiny anteaters 109–110.*
Marsupialia	At birth the young of this order are tiny. They have only started to develop. Most of the mothers have pouches. Except for opossums, these mammals are found only in Australia and neighboring islands. SOME MEMBERS: *kangaroos 57–58, koalas 59, opossums 78–79.*
Insectivora	These are small, short-legged, insect-eating mammals. SOME MEMBERS: *hedgehogs 48, moles 68–69, shrews 106.*
Dermoptera	The members of this order are squirrel-sized mammals of Southeast Asia. They are sometimes called flying lemurs, but that is not a very good name. They are not lemurs, and they cannot fly. A better name is colugo. Colugos live in trees, where they feed on leaves and fruits. They are active at night. Although they cannot fly, they glide from tree to tree. MEMBERS: *colugos, or flying lemurs*
Chiroptera	The members of this order have wings. They are the only mammals that can truly fly. MEMBERS: *bats 12–14.*
Primates	This is the order to which man belongs. Apes and monkeys also belong to it. The order contains the most intelligent of living creatures. It also contains several much less highly developed mammals. Almost all members have hands that work like man's. MEMBERS: *man, apes 6–7 (also chimpanzees 26–27, gorillas 46), monkeys 71–74 (also baboons 9–10), lower primates (tarsiers, lemurs, lorises, pottos, tree shrews) 74.*
Edentata	The mammals in this order either have no teeth or have simple, peglike teeth. MEMBERS: *anteaters 3, armadillos 8, sloths 108–109.*

Pholidota	This small order is made up of mammals armored with large, hard scales that overlap one another. The mammals defend themselves by rolling up. MEMBERS: *pangolins 83.*
Lagomorpha	The mammals in this order have two pairs of front teeth in the upper jaw. A small pair grows behind the large front pair. Most members of the order have long hind legs and long ears. MEMBERS: *pikas 86, rabbits and hares 92–94.*
Rodentia	This huge order contains about half of all the land mammals. The members are gnawing mammals, with four chisel-shaped front teeth. SOME MEMBERS: *rodents 98–99 (also beavers 17–19, chipmunks 27–28, guinea pigs 47, hamsters 47, lemmings 59–60, mice and rats 65–67, muskrats 77–78, pocket gophers 87–88, porcupines 89, prairie dogs 90, squirrels 110–112, woodchucks 123).*
Cetacea	The members of this order are water-dwelling mammals with fish-like shapes and little or no hair. MEMBERS: *dolphins 35–36, whales 117–120.*
Carnivora	This is the order of flesh-eating mammals. MEMBERS: *cats 22–24 (also cheetahs 26, jaguars 56, leopards 60, lions 61, mountain lions 75–76, tigers 114), dogs 32–34 (also coyotes 29, foxes 40–42, jackals 55–56, wolves 121–122), hyenas 54, bears 15–17, raccoons 95, coatis, and pandas 82, weasels 116 (also badgers 11, ferrets 40, martens 64–65, mink 68, otters 80–81, polecats 88, skunks 107–108, weasels 116, wolverines 120), civets 70 and mongooses 70, seals 103–104, sea lions 101–102, and walruses 115.*
Tubulidentata	This small order contains only the aardvarks. They are long-snouted, long-clawed, insect eating mammals. Their tube-shaped teeth have no roots. MEMBERS: *aardvarks 2.*
Proboscidea	Today's members are the elephants—huge mammals with trunks. MEMBERS: *elephants 37–39.*
Hyracoidea	The members are small, active mammals with hooves. MEMBERS: *hyraxes 55.*
Sirenia	The members are large, water-dwelling mammals with flippers, paddle-shaped tails, and no hind legs. MEMBERS: *sea cows 100.*
Perissodactyla	This order contains the hoofed mammals with an odd number of toes on each hind foot. MEMBERS: *horses 50-53 (also donkeys 36–37, zebras 124), rhinoceroses 97–98, tapirs 113.*
Artiodactyla	This is a large order of hoofed mammals with an even number of toes on each foot. SOME MEMBERS: *pigs 84–85, peccaries 85, and hippopotamuses 49, camels 21 and llamas 62–63, chevrotains, deer 29–31 (also moose 75, reindeer 96), giraffes 42–43, pronghorns 91, cattle-like mammals (buffaloes 20, cattle 24–25, goats 44–45, musk-oxen 76–77, Old World antelopes 4–5, sheep 105).*

Index